THE PEACE INITIATIVE
RESOURCE MANUAL

AKA Pursuing Peace – Fighting with the Judgment of Charity

A Workbook for Biblical Peacemakers

©2018 Gerhard (Gary) T. deBock

Contents

INTRODUCTION.. 7

HAVE WE EXPERIENCED SHALOM? 11

CORE COMMITMENTS 13

    PURSUE PEACE 14

    ESCALATE WITH OTHERS...15

    ACQUIRE THE JUDGMENT OF CHARITY 16

    CHOOSE TRUE FORGIVENESS...17

    EXPECT ACCOUNTABILITY 19

    GRAPHIC: DETOURS & BACKTRACKING 20

BIBLICAL FOUNDATIONS 21

    PURSUE PEACE 23

    ESCALATE WITH OTHERS...35

    ACQUIRE THE JUDGMENT OF CHARITY 39

    CHOOSE TRUE FORGIVENESS...45

    EXPECT ACCOUNTABILITY 49

ONE-PAGE TRAINING SHEETS 53

    JUDGMENT OF CHARITY..54

    JUDGMENT OF CHARITY VERSUS THE BENEFIT OF THE DOUBT ...55

    E.L.M...56

    CARE-FRONTING..57

    1 CORINTHIANS 13 LOVE..58

    HOW WE TREAT JESUS 59

    CHANGING ME – INFLUENCING YOU 60

    UNDERSTANDING, NOT EXCUSING 61

    CAN TRUST BE REBUILT WITHOUT THE JUDGMENT OF CHARITY?.....62

    MUST WE TRI? MORE THAN ONCE? 63

    WHEN TO JUDGE 64

    MOTIVES & METHODS 65

SPEAK THE TRUTH IN LOVE 66

COMMUNICATION FILTERS 67

MIND-READING & PIGEON-HOLING 68

STOP, LOOK, AND LISTEN 69

GOSSIP 70

HEARSAY 71

REPENTANCE VERSUS FRUITS OF REPENTANCE 72

CYCLE OF CONFLICT 73

INCREASING TENSION'S IMPACTS through the stages of conflict 74

GRAPHIC: IMPACTS OF THE CYCLE 75

SOMETHING'S WRONG Stage One in the Cycle of Conflict 76

WHAT'S WRONG Stage Two in the Cycle of Conflict 77

YOU'RE WRONG Stage Three in the Cycle of Conflict.......................78

LET'S FIGHT! Stage Four in the Cycle of Conflict 79

WHO WON? Stage Five in the Cycle of Conflict 80

GRAPHIC: CYCLE OF CONFLICT WITH LABELS 81

INJUSTICE GATHERING..82

THE DEATH SPIRAL and the Cycle of Conflict 83

THE DEATH SPIRAL A Self-Assessment..84

TWO TENSIONS OF CONFLICT 85

FIVE STYLES OF CONFLICT RESOLUTION 86

TURTLES...87

TEDDY BEARS...88

SHARKS 89

FOXES 90

OWLS 91

ASSESSING MY CONFLICT STYLES...92

SCORING YOUR CONFLICT STYLES ASSESSMENT 93

WHAT WE CONTROL MOST IN CONFLICT 94

THE TROUBLE WITH TURTLES 95

THE TROUBLE WITH TEDDY BEARS 96

THE TROUBLE WITH SHARKS..97

THE TROUBLE WITH FOXES 98

THE BENEFITS OF OWLS 99

"MELT-MOLD-MAKE FIRM"..100

TWO HANDS OF FORGIVENESS: GOD AND PEOPLE 101

TWO HANDS OF FORGIVENESS: DIAGRAMMED 102

TWO HANDS OF FORGIVENESS: APPLIED TO OUR RELATIONSHIPS 103

THE MAP OF FORGIVENESS: LEFT SIDE 104

THE MAP OF FORGIVENESS: RIGHT SIDE 105

FORGIVENESS: A DECISION AND A PROCESS 106

A GOOD APOLOGY 107

LEAVE ROOM FOR THE VENGEANCE OF GOD 108

THROW THE ROPE DOWN THE HOLE 109

FORGIVENESS QUESTIONS & ANSWERS: Head 110

FORGIVENESS QUESTIONS & ANSWERS: Heart 112

"DO I HAVE TO FORGIVE GOD?" 114

"DO I NEED TO FORGIVE MYSELF?" 115

FALSE FORGIVENESS = NO PEACE 116

CHECKLIST: WHEN WE HAVE CONFLICT 117

CHECKLIST: WHEN OTHERS HAVE CONFLICT 119

SINS AND RESENTMENT LISTS: A TOOL 121

"TIME-OUT!" 122

WHY TAKE NOTES? 123

"I JUST NEED TIME AND SPACE." 124

HAVE I LOST THE JUDGMENT OF CHARITY? 125

GENTLENESS-MEEKNESS ASSESSMENT 127

PRAYERS FOR RESTORING THE JUDGMENT OF CHARITY 128

MEDIATION TRIAGE – Three Session Instructions............................ 129

SESSION ONE 129

SESSION TWO 133

SESSION THREE 135

MEDIATOR TRIAGE WORKSHEETS 137

CASE STUDIES 143

INSTRUCTIONS 144

CASE STUDY 1 145

CASE STUDY 2 147

CASE STUDY 3 149

CASE STUDY 4 151

CASE STUDY 5 153

CASE STUDY 6 155

CASE STUDY 7 157

CASE STUDY 8 159

CASE STUDY 9 161

CASE STUDY 10 163

CASE STUDY 11 165

CASE STUDY 12 167

CASE STUDY 13 169

CASE STUDY 14 171

CASE STUDY 15 173

CASE STUDY 16 175

GLOSSARY FOR CASE STUDIES 177

WORKSHOP PREPARATION INSTRUCTIONS **185**

ADDITIONAL DISCUSSION QUESTIONS **187**

SELECT BIBLIOGRAPHY **189**

> **Finally, brothers, rejoice.**
> **Aim for restoration,**
> **comfort one another,**
> **agree with one another,**
> **live in peace;**
> **and the God of love and peace**
> **will be with you.**
>
> *2 Corinthians 13:11*

INTRODUCTION

"Would you please teach an adult class on conflict management?" Thirty-five years ago, all I could say was, "Not right now. I don't know a thing about the subject. But, if you give me a year, I'll go and see what I can learn that might be useful."

So, as a young pastor I began a time of intense study. I learned from Norm Shawchuck about the five animal styles of dealing with conflict. Insights were gained into the cycle of conflict and the tools of resolution. Twelve months or so later, I taught the class. It was well received and through some university staff in our church I was asked to teach the material to fifty key faculty and staff leaders. Since then I have taught the material at retreats, in seminars, workshops and one-on-one.

Over the past thirty-four years, the challenge has become far greater than just keeping people's interest. Everyone likes to learn about the styles and communication filters. Even the cycle of conflict can hold folks' attention. No, the challenge is how to help people CHANGE how they deal with conflict and its aftermath.

A few years into my journey, I did another season of focused study. This time it was on the biblical theology of forgiveness. Seeking to welcome all the biblical input available, I realized that our misunderstanding of this vital topic has left many Christians either in abusive situations OR feeling like they must leave the situation. The Body of Christ, especially local churches, bear the scars of un-confronted sin or divisive abandonment.

The peace that God wants us to have in our relationships, especially in the local church between brothers and sisters in Christ, is one of wholeness and harmony. It is much more than merely the absence of outward conflict because we refuse to face it. Or because we just leave. The peace that we can now have through Jesus' Christ's work in His life, death, and resurrection is the model, the benchmark for the peace we are to have with each other.

My own experiences with conflict have left me with tender scars that prickle each time they are touched. I ache wondering why these folks had to leave. Why could that marriage not be saved? After all, we are talking about professing Christians, who say they have all the resources of the Holy Spirit Who indwells them.

Have We Experienced SHALOM?

Can anything turn the tide of Christians who are comfortable being on their third, fourth, and even fifth church, all within a local region? What can change the divorce rate among Christians so that it no longer equals or exceeds the pace at which non-churchgoers separate?

It makes sense that we cannot give what we have not received. We cannot share what we have not experienced. **Perhaps the most foundational reason that we do not pursue peace is that we have not known peace,** especially that strong peace that is call SHALOM in the Old Testament. The next section in this workbook is designed to stir a yearning within us, or a remembrance back to, our experience of SHALOM with God through Christ.

I have come to believe that for us to truly pursue peace it will take a God-sent revival. This awakening will first be about our experiencing the Prince of Peace personally. Then, it will need to cascade into a Holy Spirit empowered repentance and faith to welcome the truth of God's Word and apply it. Specifically, I think it will take a wholehearted embracing of five core commitments, spelling out PEACE. The first two are the most difficult.

An Overview of the Five Commitments

The commitment to **Pursue peace** is first. This means that we can no longer tolerate within ourselves a passivity about unity and relational peace. Nor can we continue to cozy up to accepting division in the Body of Christ like it is normal and OK.

Even harder that this will be the second commitment. To humble ourselves enough to pursue peace by being **willing to Escalate care-fronting (caring enough to confront), even if it means getting the help of others.** We will find it very difficult to drive these two vital tent pegs into the rock-hard soil of our sinful individualism. For too many, if not most of us, our individual decisions and perceived needs trump the authority and importance of the local church. Biblically, the family is very important but the way we idolize family over our commitment to the Body of Christ keeps us from experiencing peace. We just keep running away or verbally gunning down others, instead of following our Savior's clear teachings.

Having taught this material for nearly three and a half decades, I have realized that without these first two commitments, the last three probably will make little difference. The third through fifth commitments are more about practical how-to.

The third critical step to pursuing peace is to be firmly determined to **Acquire the Judgment of Charity.** Without this, we will not be acting out of love, becoming noisy gongs. Another advance in pursuing peace will be the setting of our jaws to **Choose true forgiveness.** Not the world's kind of forgiveness that is more about us feeling better. Rather, God's kind of forgiveness that is strong and makes a way for there to be real reconciliation. Lastly, real change will demand that we are firm and **Expect accountability** – talk of change is not enough, there must be verifiable fruit.

The Workbook is Designed for Flexibility

This training material is laid out so that you can choose how you learn best. If you are not convinced of the five commitments, then learn more about them. Dig through the Scriptures and see if the foundation for these commitments is biblical.

Do you do better when you have the overview of all the major concepts? Then work through the one-page training sheets. You can fly through them using the summary thoughts in the sidebar box at the top. Dig a bit deeper by reading the body of the page. Then check your work by thinking through the pop quizzes.

Perhaps you learn best by getting thrown into the deep end. Jump right in to the case studies. The glossary at the end can help you with terms and concepts (as will referring to the one-page training sheets). Do not cheat by skipping the part where you write your own notes on what should/could be done. Then, after you have done some thinking, check out Gary's thoughts. Even better, work through these case studies with a small group.

Test yourself by using the assessment tools sprinkled throughout the one-page training sheets. Why not try to go through the Mediation Triage Tool with your spouse or someone with whom you are in a relationship? If it gets too tough, remember to seek help. If the relationship is troubled or fragile, please seek outside help to go through the three sessions.

A fantastic way to grow is in a workshop with an experienced mediator. Submit your own case study (with names and identifiers removed or replaced). Then, work through how to apply the concepts while living out the five commitments.

<u>My Prayer for Us</u>

May the Prince of Peace allow us to experience through the blood of Jesus' cross the peace with God that leaves us rejoicing. May Jesus, Who is our peace, grant us to remember the consolation, comfort, affection, sympathy, and encouragement that we have received. **May the Spirit stir us to want to share with others the SHALOM we have received.**

May our gracious Lord help us to pursue peace with others, even as He pursued it with us.

P – Pursue Peace

E – Escalate with Help

A – Acquire the Judgment of Charity

C – Choose True Forgiveness

E – Expect Accountability

HAVE WE EXPERIENCED SHALOM?

The Hebrew concept of **SHALOM enriches our sense of what peace really is.** It has a range of meaning that includes the opposite of war, the well-being that comes from God, prosperity, bodily health, contentedness, salvation, good relations between nations and men, wholeness, completion, and harmony. We can have this peace with God, within ourselves, and with others.

The Apostle Paul challenges the Philippians and us to be unified, not looking out for our own interests but rather serving others. His foundation for this call to practiced-in-daily-life love is **based on what we have already experienced as believers.**

> *So if there is any encouragement in Christ, any comfort from love, any participation in the Spirit, any affection and sympathy, complete my joy by being of the same mind, having the same love, being in full accord and of one mind. – Philippians 2:1-2*

He assumes that there has already been encouragement, comfort, participation, affection, and sympathy. In the same way, for us to be those who pursue peace, in the fullest sense of the word, we must already have experienced peace. **We cannot give what we have not received. We cannot share what we have not experienced.**

The peace we have with God comes through Jesus. He Himself is our peace. He has made peace, between us and God and between us and other believers.

> *For in him all the fullness of God was pleased to dwell, and through him to reconcile to himself all things, whether on earth or in heaven, **making peace by the blood of his cross**. – Colossians 1:19-20*

> *But now in Christ Jesus you who once were far off have been brought near by the blood of Christ. **For he himself is our peace**, who has made us both one and has broken down in his flesh the dividing wall of hostility by abolishing the law of commandments expressed in ordinances, that he might create in himself one new man in place of the two, **so making peace**, and might reconcile us both to God in one body through the cross, thereby killing the hostility. – Ephesians 2:13-16*

When, through our faith in Jesus Christ and His work on the cross, we experience Shalom, then this peace is also *within* us. It **rules our hearts** (Colossians 3:16). This peace of God is so strong that as we pray we find that the peace **"surpasses all understanding"** and **guards our hearts and minds.** This experience is first ours after we have been born again. It continues to be ours as we are daily filled with the Spirit of God, keeping in step with Him and manifesting His fruit, including peace (Galatians 5:22).

<u>If we have experienced SHALOM, we will want others to experience it as well.</u>

The joy of knowing that we have been justified, declared righteous, by God through Christ is a powerful incentive. We find a joy that delights so much in God that even when we are facing suffering we still rejoice in God. We are confident that He will work all things together for our good and His glory (Romans 8:28).

> *Therefore, since we have been justified by faith, **we have peace with God through our Lord Jesus Christ.** Through him we have also obtained access by faith into this grace in which we stand, and we rejoice in hope of the glory of God. Not only that, but **we rejoice in our sufferings** . . . – Romans 5:1-3a*

I believe this SHALOM, or oneness, that we experience is what Jesus prayed about. His prayer makes it clear **that our experience of SHALOM with God and with other believers is essential for us to be effective witnesses**, as we have been commissioned to be.

> *"I do not ask for these only, but also for those who will believe in me through their word, that they may all be one, just as you, Father, are in me, and I in you, that they also may be in us, **so that the world may believe that you have sent me.**"*

> *"I in them and you in me, that they may become perfectly one, **so that the world may know that you sent me and loved them even as you loved me.**" – John 17:20-21, 23*

Those who have experienced SHALOM will yearn for others to have the same experience. We will find joy and strength in living out the commands of Scripture regarding our relationship with others. Though imperfectly until our Lord returns, because we have known the peace He gives, **we want to be like Him and be a peacemaker.** Our peace is not as the world gives, but of the highest order of God's SHALOM.

> *"Peace I leave with you; my peace I give to you. **Not as the world gives do I give to you**. Let not your hearts be troubled, neither let them be afraid." – John 14:27*

> *"Blessed are the peacemakers, **for they shall be called sons of God.**" – Matthew 5:9*

Because we rejoice in all God has done for us through our Savior and the Spirit, we joyful engage in pursuing peace.

> *Finally, brothers, rejoice. Aim for restoration, comfort one another, agree with one another, **live in peace**; and the God of love and peace will be with you. – 2 Corinthians 13:11*

CORE COMMITMENTS

Over the years, as I have taught this material in many contexts, I have marveled at how so many try to wiggle out of the biblical pattern taught to us. As I have fought for the Judgment of Charity on behalf of these individuals and couples, I have concluded that most of them are not really convinced that God's pattern applies to them.

We must firmly hold to five core commitments if we are to push through the challenges of handling conflict God's way. A weak "head nod" toward any one of them will spell trouble down the road. These beliefs are summarized by the following phrases:

Pursue Peace
Escalate with Others
Acquire the Judgment of Charity
Choose True Forgiveness
Expect Accountability

Without a strong commitment to the biblical mandate to **PURSUE PEACE,** it is too easy for us to avoid conflicts or accommodate others out of our neediness. We can easily slip into trying to control others with our assertiveness or our negotiation skills. More than a few of us will give up on our marriages, our churches, or our friends.

Without a firm sense of our obligation to **ESCALATE WITH OTHERS,** the clear majority of us will never seek the help of others in conflict. We may vent our feelings or try to get people to jump on our bandwagon, but truly being open to others helping us mediate conflict, even to the point of submission to their arbitration, is too much for us if we are only fair-weather fans of Christ.

Without setting our faces like flint toward **ACQUIRING THE JUDGMENT OF CHARITY,** we will fool ourselves into thinking that we are objective judges about the conflicts we are embroiled in. Our anger and even bitterness will so cloud our thinking and how we express ourselves, that true biblical peace often will sail off to the horizon.

Without the "loving much of the one who has been forgiven much" (see Luke 7:41-47) undergirding our commitment to **CHOOSE TRUE FORGIVENESS,** we will be stuck being judgmental of imperfect people. Our filters, still clogged by hurt and anger, will not let us cover a multitude of sins with love.

Finally, if we do not firmly believe that we should **EXPECT ACCOUNTABILITY** for our promises, or if we are unwilling to hold others accountable to theirs, we will find ourselves embracing a "cheap forgiveness." Weak forgiveness has no connection to the repentance of changed hearts that is worked out into the fruits of repentance of changed lives.

> *I encourage you to review these five commitments. The simple Bible study that follows, after the review of the Core Commitments, will guide you to some of the many passages that present instruction about God's will for us in these areas. Some of these passages will give us biblical examples of these commitments and their consequences.*

PURSUE PEACE

Jesus teaches us: "Blessed are the peacemakers, for they shall be called sons of God.[1] Our Savior prays for our unity, to be at the level of the unity of the Father and the Son.[2] He instructs us to initiate the steps toward reconciliation with those who have sinned against us[3] and those who we know have something against us.[4]

Jesus' apostles direct us to be at peace with all men, as much as it depends on us.[5] And to pursue peace,[6] forgiving others as we have been forgiven by God through Christ.[7] We are warned again and again about the dangers of division in the body of Christ, especially within the local church.[8]

<u>What keeps us from pursuing peace?</u> The common denominator to our excuses seems to be **fear**. We are afraid of conflict. Anxious that our weaknesses will be exposed. We dread the unknown and potentially uncontrollable. We choose to stay within our comfortable posture of hiding in self-defense or hurling blame, even though neither has ever gotten us what we really desire. We are more afraid rather than full of faith to obey our Master's desires and directives.

Until we are convinced by the Scriptures and the Spirit that we are mandated to pursue peace, we will probably continue to look for ways to be in control, avoiding or minimizing conflict when possible. If we are convinced of our mandate, we will submit to the Spirit's control over our actions and reactions as we face the tension of conflict.

☐ *Do I believe that I am mandated by Jesus to be an initiator in pursuing peace, especially in my relationships with other believers?*

---

[1] Matthew 5:9
[2] John 17:20-21
[3] Matthew 18:15
[4] Matthew 5:23-24
[5] Romans 12:18
[6] Hebrews 12:14
[7] Ephesians 4:32
[8] For example: Galatians 5:14-15, 1 Corinthians 3:1-4

ESCALATE WITH OTHERS

If we embrace the first core belief, that we are mandated to pursue peace, we still can fall short of being a true biblical peacemaker. Most people want peace and are willing to make <u>some</u> attempts at pursuing it. These efforts are better than not trying at all, but *pursuing peace* requires a Christ-follower to be willing to escalate the care-fronting (caring enough to confront). We must believe that God calls us to pursue peace with such vigor that we will be willing to ask others to help us as we escalate our care-fronting.[9]

Jesus teaches us to begin one-on-one. If this least-threat-level effort does not result in peace, we are to escalate things. Matthew 18 teaches us to next take one or two witnesses and, if need be, to be willing to take it to the gathered assembly of believers.

The Apostle Paul teaches us the same concept, but with leaders the escalation should happen even more quickly.[10] He also instructs us to be willing to submit to binding arbitration rather than the horror of our unresolved conflict bringing slander to the name of Jesus.[11]

<u>What keeps us from desiring peace enough to ask for help</u>? Why do we give up after trying it on our own to fix our marriage or our relationship with other believers? As hard as it is to admit, behind this unwillingness to escalate, especially with the help of others, is *pride.* We don't want others to know about our problems. We recoil from the thought of someone else directing the process of reconciliation. We are too egotistical to submit to the authority of church leaders within the local assembly.

True peacemakers are humble. They are willing to bend the knee to Christ by submitting to His teachings. They are subject to the appropriate and Christ-instituted authority of the local church. They are willing to escalate. And they are willing to ask for help.

☐ *Do I believe that my pursuit of peace is so important that I will go through the pain of escalating it, even when it means asking others to help me?*

---

[9] Matthew 18:15-17
[10] 1 Timothy 5:19-21
[11] 1 Corinthians 6:1-8

ACQUIRE THE JUDGMENT OF CHARITY

Until the Judgment of Charity is restored to a significant level, most of our efforts pursuing a lasting and true peace will fail. Any measure of reconciliation that does not include the restoration of the Judgment of Charity is only a veneer of peace. It does not adequately reflect what Jesus died to give us, true peace with God.

The Judgment of Charity is the decision of the will to actively think from God's perspective regarding another person's motives. It is the active choice to seek a verdict regarding another person's motives in the court of God's love. We give someone the judgment of love, rather than bitterness, when we assume the best possible motives for the other person's methods.

If pride keeps us from asking for and submitting to help, it also sets us up to imagine that we have a right to hang on to our *anger*. We allow ourselves to imagine that restoring the Judgment of Charity is only a bonus blessing. It is nice to have but not essential to lasting peace.

Romans 5 tells us of our relationship with God and so shines a light on what true peace is like. Biblical peace leaves us rejoicing in the other party, even at the thought of them coming to a position of power, with authority to judge us and our work. It even rejoices in our suffering, when we do not really understand the other person's methods. That is because we trust their motives, that they truly love us. Biblical peace enables us to give the Judgment of Charity.[12] The peace we have with God is the standard for the peace we pursue with others, especially other believers.

We all tend to give ourselves the Judgment of Charity. Because of this, it takes humility to admit that we are not able to be the final judge of even our own hearts. We can seek to live with a clear conscience, but even that is not an objective guarantee of our righteous innocence.[13]

We even yearn for others to give us the Judgment of Charity, assuming about us that our intentions are good, even when our methods get messed up. Most of us struggle to hear critique of our methods. But, even the most open among us, when we perceive someone is attacking our motives, will quickly raise our defenses. We want others to give us the Judgment of Charity.

So, we must do unto others what we want them to do to us. We must seek, with the Spirit's help, to acquire the Judgment of Charity. The true peacemaker understands that peace is deeper than the absence of conflict. Making sure we do not see the other party again may reduce the outward occurrences and pain of conflict, but it does nothing to restore peace. Rather, we must seek the presence of a wholeness and a harmony that comes because we truly trust the other person again.[14] Without the restoration of the Judgment of Charity, there is no chance for trust to be rebuilt.

☐ *Do I believe that I should not just work through the methods in the conflict, but all the way to the heart of the matter, seeking the restoration of the Judgment of Charity?*

---

[12] Romans 5:1-11 speaks of three ways peace with God leaves us rejoicing
[13] 1 Corinthians 4:3-5
[14] Peace is referring to the Old Testament concept of Shalom. This wholeness and harmony is much more than just the absence of conflict or enemies.

CHOOSE TRUE FORGIVENESS

Once convinced of the need to actively seek the restoration of the Judgment of Charity, the question becomes, "How?" If we imagine that peace will come from blaming others or defending ourselves, we remain in the grip of *bitterness.* In humility we may even ask for help, as we escalate the conflict. But, what has the power to *deeply heal* the hurts of wrongs done and "rights" left undone?

Since we cannot go back in time and change the past, even physical restitution will not "fix" things at the heart level. Yes, "making things right" shows the outward fruit of inward repentance. But, it rarely can fully restore the Judgment of Charity. We often feel like the other party is making changes, but not out of good motives. Perhaps they are "changing" but only out of the pressure of the confrontation. This is especially true if others have been brought in to the situation as witnesses or mediators. What happens when the pressure goes away? Will they just revert?

We deceive ourselves when we think the Judgment of Charity does not matter to the future of the relationship. When it is lost or even weakened, our filters are set to pick up on the future "mistakes" of the other person. We will not be looking for them to change for the good. Rather, we will subtly slip back into a form of injustice gathering, scouring their actions for evidence that they really did *not* change.

Love covers a multitude of sins.[15] But when love is absent we nit-pick and assume the worst. How can we restore the Judgment of Charity without the other party first "rebuilding trust" through perfect behavior? How can we open our filters in hope, rather than close them in bitterness? Imperfect humans, who will sin again, cannot "earn" their way back into another's good grace. No one will score a 100%, and if our filters are set to find the flaws, how can there be peace?

The good news is that the Judgment of Charity can be restored by choosing to extend biblical forgiveness to others. Yet we must remember that while we are called to extend forgiveness to all, we only forgive (in the completed sense that allows for reconciliation) those who have repented. Without owning what a person did or failed to do in the past (repentance), the full restoration of forgiveness is impossible.

Without extending forgiveness in the hope of reconciliation, our closed fists of bitterness will continue to cloud our judgment. We may think we are being wise judges, but we are merely being judgmental.

The biblical teaching on repentance and forgiveness is easily twisted into making it all about our feeling better by "letting it go." Such "cheap forgiveness," that does not at least seek reconciliation, is an expression of our desire to "feel better." We yearn not to be prisoners of our own "hate" and bitterness. So, we "forgive," all the while continuing to hold the others' sins against them by refusing to be in a meaningful relationship with them.

---

[15] Proverbs 10:12; 1 Peter 4:8

We are called to extend forgiveness to all. But, we forgive only those who have repented.[16] And, with a measure of the Judgment of Charity restored, we root for them to rebuild trust by manifesting the fruits of repentance.

☐ *Do I believe that biblical forgiveness is essential to the restoration of the Judgment of Charity, which is needful in the pursuit of the peace of reconciliation?*

---

[16] Luke 17:3-4

EXPECT ACCOUNTABILITY

Some do not want to talk about the connection between repentance and forgiveness. They think if we embrace grace then we cannot hold people accountable for their future actions (or inactions). None of us wants to get hurt again. So, understandably, we want to be able to hold the other person accountable. But, our distorted view of forgiveness leads us to believe that we will *not* be able to do that.

Forgiveness deals with the past sins of commission and omission. Completed forgiveness, or reconciliation, requires that the erring party express repentance. Because repentance is a change of heart that only God can see, we *by faith* and in obedience to Jesus' teachings, forgive them based on their claim to repentance. We would rather not walk by faith. Rather, we would *like* to wait until the fruits of repentance, which we *can* see with our eyes, manifest themselves over time. But this desire takes us back to the previous core commitment. Without the restoration of the Judgment of Charity, no one will ever get 100% on the "fruits of repentance test." And the Judgment of Charity can only be restored through choosing forgiveness.

The biblical peacemaker understands that forgiveness is what restores the Judgment of Charity. And that the fruits of repentance, for which we are held accountable after forgiveness has been extended, rebuild trust. But, without the Judgment of Charity, even a healthy score of 90% on the manifested fruits of repentance test will leave us bitter. *"How could they fail 10% of the time if they were serious about repentance?!"* The Judgment of Charity will allow us to pray and root for the other person as they make progress in working out their heart's repentance into their lives.

Expecting accountability is not about demanding perfection. This "perfect" standard is not one that we ourselves want to be held to. We say, *"Can't you see that I'm really trying?! I did all these things right and all you can focus on is this?"* Unfortunately, we often do not see the hypocrisy of using one measure on others while wanting them to use a different one us.[17] By restoring the Judgment of Charity, based on an expression of repentance, we can now use a large measure of grace to hold others lovingly accountable for the manifestation of the fruits of repentance.

As conflict escalates, others will become the judge of whether the repeat offender is merely mouthing the words of repentance. They will be the ones to decide if he is to be treated as an unbeliever.[18] Even then, we can love our enemies knowing that they do not have the Holy Spirit to help them live differently. This maintains the Judgment of Charity about our enemies' motives, while keeping them accountable for their visible methods.

> ☐ *Do I believe that people should be held accountable to manifest the fruits of repentance in the future, but that my forgiveness of their past sins is tied to their declaration of repentance?*

---

[17] Matthew 7:1-2
[18] Matthew 18:17-20

GRAPHIC: DETOURS & BACKTRACKING

DETOURS AND BACKTRACKING WHILE PURSUING PEACE

Taking a "detour" often leads to backtracking into previous dead ends

- The help we seek is only to allow us to "vent."
- Or to seek support in our blaming of the other party.
- Or to seek pity for our pain.

- "Forgiveness" is only about me feeling better.
- "I've forgiven them but I won't be reconciled with them!"
- "If I forgive them then I have to let them continue to hurt me."

Assume because we tried we are no longer responsible

ACQUIRE THE JUDGMENT OF CHARITY

CHOOSE TRUE FORGIVENESS

ESCALATE WITH HELP

PEACE

EXPECT ACCOUNT-ABILITY

- "I forgive them but I won't allow trust to be rebuilt through the fruits of repentance."
- "I demand that they deserve my grace. They will have to earn my trust with 100% perfection."

PURSUE PEACE

- Abdicate our responsibility
- Remain in abusive relationship
- Abandon the relationship

UNRESOLVED CONFLICT

BIBLICAL FOUNDATIONS

The CORE COMMITMENTS are essential for pressing through the challenges of pursuing peace. They are grounded in God's Word, the Bible. The following section will take you through several texts and ask you to reflect on them. If you are not familiar with the context, grab your Bible and make sure you are looking for the author's intention.

While the sections within this study fall into the outline of the five CORE COMMITMENTS, many of the passages could be used to support several of the commitments. The goal is not that you agree with my outline but that you would gain a firm grasp on the biblical foundations for becoming a peacemaker.

**Come, O children, listen to me;
I will teach you the fear of the Lord.
What man is there who desires life
and loves many days,
that he may see good?
Keep your tongue from evil
and your lips from speaking deceit.
Turn away from evil and do good;
seek peace and pursue it.**

Psalms 34:11-14

PURSUE PEACE

Read the following passages and jot down your notes on the answers to the guiding questions. The texts start out focused on the general commands to pursue peace and God's example of doing so. We then will notice what is God's ideal for relationships in the local church. We will read of the call to be initiators in the pursuit of peace. Finally, we will work through several generally related texts. A place to capture notes on other scriptural references the Lord brings to your mind is provided at the end of the section.

1 Corinthians 13:4 Love is patient and kind; love does not envy or boast; it is not arrogant [5]or rude. It does not insist on its own way; it is not irritable or resentful; [6]it does not rejoice at wrongdoing but rejoices with the truth. [7]Love bears all things, believes all things, hopes all things, endures all things.	*How does the Apostle Paul's definition of love correlate with your understanding of the Judgment of Charity?*
John 17:20 "I do not ask for these only, but also for those who will believe in me through their word, [21]that they may all be one, just as you, Father, are in me, and I in you, that they also may be in us, so that the world may believe that you have sent me. [22]The glory that you have given me I have given to them, that they may be one even as we are one, [23]I in them and you in me, that they may become perfectly one, so that the world may know that you sent me and loved them even as you loved me.	*What is Jesus' desire for the church?* *Why is this Father-Son-like unity so important?* *What does division between believers communicate to the world?*
Isaiah 58:12 And your ancient ruins shall be rebuilt; you shall raise up the foundations of many generations; you shall be called the repairer of the breach, the restorer of streets to dwell in.	*God is willing to restore His people even after great failure. What would be another title we could give to a peacemaker?*

23

Psalm 85:10 Steadfast love and faithfulness meet; righteousness and peace kiss each other.	*The psalmist expresses hope that God will revive His people. What are the four components of this wonderful "nexus" of hope?*
John 1:14 And the Word became flesh and dwelt among us, and we have seen his glory, glory as of the only Son from the Father, full of grace and truth. ¹⁵(John bore witness about him, and cried out, "This was he of whom I said, 'He who comes after me ranks before me, because he was before me.'") ¹⁶For from his fullness we have all received, grace upon grace. ¹⁷For the law was given through Moses; grace and truth came through Jesus Christ. ¹⁸No one has ever seen God; the only God, who is at the Father's side, he has made him known.	*God is the initiator Who pursues peace with us. He sent His Son. How is Jesus the perfect balance of what is needed to find peace in our relationship with God?*
Jeremiah 36:1 In the fourth year of Jehoiakim the son of Josiah, king of Judah, this word came to Jeremiah from the Lord: ²"Take a scroll and write on it all the words that I have spoken to you against Israel and Judah and all the nations, from the day I spoke to you, from the days of Josiah until today. ³It may be that the house of Judah will hear all the disaster that I intend to do to them, so that everyone may turn from his evil way, and that I may forgive their iniquity and their sin."	*Even at the worst times, God's posture is one of care-fronting His people. What is His heart's desire behind His strong rebuke?*

Matthew 5:38 "You have heard that it was said, 'An eye for an eye and a tooth for a tooth.' [39]But I say to you, Do not resist the one who is evil. But if anyone slaps you on the right cheek, turn to him the other also. [40]And if anyone would sue you and take your tunic, let him have your cloak as well. [41]And if anyone forces you to go one mile, go with him two miles. [42]Give to the one who begs from you, and do not refuse the one who would borrow from you. [43]"You have heard that it was said, 'You shall love your neighbor and hate your enemy.' [44]But I say to you, Love your enemies and pray for those who persecute you, [45]so that you may be sons of your Father who is in heaven. For he makes his sun rise on the evil and on the good, and sends rain on the just and on the unjust. [46]For if you love those who love you, what reward do you have? Do not even the tax collectors do the same? [47]And if you greet only your brothers, what more are you doing than others? Do not even the Gentiles do the same? [48]You therefore must be perfect, as your heavenly Father is perfect.

Jesus' directives for us challenge us to at least fight for the Judgment of Charity in our relationships. How is this like turning the other cheek, going the extra mile, and loving our enemies?

Romans 12:14 Bless those who persecute you; bless and do not curse them. [15]Rejoice with those who rejoice, weep with those who weep. [16]Live in harmony with one another. Do not be haughty, but associate with the lowly. Never be wise in your own sight. [17]Repay no one evil for evil, but give thought to do what is honorable in the sight of all. [18]If possible, so far as it depends on you, live peaceably with all. [19]Beloved, never avenge yourselves, but leave it to the wrath of God, for it is written, "Vengeance is mine, I will repay, says the Lord." [20]To the contrary, "if your enemy is hungry, feed him; if he is thirsty, give him something to drink; for by so doing you will heap burning coals on his head." [21]Do not be overcome by evil, but overcome evil with good.

Verse 18 challenges us to do what?

How is this command realistic in recognizing that we rarely control everything needed for peace in our relationships?

How are we to entrust ultimate judgment to God?

Hebrews 12:12 Therefore lift your drooping hands and strengthen your weak knees, [13]and make straight paths for your feet, so that what is lame may not be put out of joint but rather be healed. [14]Strive for peace with everyone, and for the holiness without which no one will see the Lord. [15]See to it that no one fails to obtain the grace of God; that no "root of bitterness" springs up and causes trouble, and by it many become defiled; [16]that no one is sexually immoral or unholy like Esau, who sold his birthright for a single meal. [17]For you know that afterward, when he desired to inherit the blessing, he was rejected, for he found no chance to repent, though he sought it with tears.	*Are we mandated to strive for peace? Why?*
Philippians 2:1 So if there is any encouragement in Christ, any comfort from love, any participation in the Spirit, any affection and sympathy, [2]complete my joy by being of the same mind, having the same love, being in full accord and of one mind. [3]Do nothing from selfish ambition or conceit, but in humility count others more significant than yourselves. [4]Let each of you look not only to his own interests, but also to the interests of others.	*What do healthy relationships between Christians look like?* *What are the motivations God gives us to pursue such relationships?*
Matthew 5:7 "Blessed are the merciful, for they shall receive mercy. [8]"Blessed are the pure in heart, for they shall see God. [9]Blessed are the peacemakers, for they shall be called sons of God."	*In Jesus' beatitudes, why are peacemakers called the sons of God? How are those who pursue peace like God?*

1 Peter 3:10 For "Whoever desires to love life and see good days, let him keep his tongue from evil and his lips from speaking deceit; [11]let him turn away from evil and do good; let him seek peace and pursue it. [12]For the eyes of the Lord are on the righteous, and his ears are open to their prayer. But the face of the Lord is against those who do evil." *(Peter is referring to Psalm 34:12-16)*	*Are we mandated to pursue peace? How is our prayer life's effectiveness tied to this pursuit?*
Romans 14:19 So then let us pursue what makes for peace and for mutual upbuilding.	*In the context of not judging our "weaker brothers," what must we set as our goal?*
1 Corinthians 3:1 But I, brothers, could not address you as spiritual people, but as people of the flesh, as infants in Christ. [2]I fed you with milk, not solid food, for you were not ready for it. And even now you are not yet ready, [3]for you are still of the flesh. For while there is jealousy and strife among you, are you not of the flesh and behaving only in a human way? [4]For when one says, "I follow Paul," and another, "I follow Apollos," are you not being merely human?	*Unresolved conflict between Christians tells us what?*
1 Corinthians 1:10 I appeal to you, brothers, by the name of our Lord Jesus Christ, that all of you agree, and that there be no divisions among you, but that you be united in the same mind and the same judgment.	*Is division within the local church the will of God?*

Colossians 3:12 Put on then, as God's chosen ones, holy and beloved, compassionate hearts, kindness, humility, meekness, and patience, [13]bearing with one another and, if one has a complaint against another, forgiving each other; as the Lord has forgiven you, so you also must forgive. [14]And above all these put on love, which binds everything together in perfect harmony. [15]And let the peace of Christ rule in your hearts, to which indeed you were called in one body. And be thankful.	*What is God's desire for our relationships with other believers, especially in the local church?* *How would you correlate what we are told to "put on" in verses 12-13 with your understanding of the Judgment of Charity?* *How does peace in our hearts relate to peace in our relationships with other Christians?*
Ephesians 4:1 I therefore, a prisoner for the Lord, urge you to walk in a manner worthy of the calling to which you have been called, [2]with all humility and gentleness, with patience, bearing with one another in love, [3]eager to maintain the unity of the Spirit in the bond of peace. [4]There is one body and one Spirit— just as you were called to the one hope that belongs to your call— [5]one Lord, one faith, one baptism, [6]one God and Father of all, who is over all and through all and in all.	*What relationship dynamics are included in walking in a manner worthy of our calling?*
Ephesians 4:15 Rather, speaking the truth in love, we are to grow up in every way into him who is the head, into Christ, [16]from whom the whole body, joined and held together by every joint with which it is equipped, when each part is working properly, makes the body grow so that it builds itself up in love.	*If we want the kind of unity God desires in the church, how must we speak to one another?*

1 Thessalonians 5:12 We ask you, brothers, to respect those who labor among you and are over you in the Lord and admonish you, [13]and to esteem them very highly in love because of their work. Be at peace among yourselves.	*What words are used to describe our relationship with church leaders and those in the local church body?*
Ezekiel 33:7 "So you, son of man, I have made a watchman for the house of Israel. Whenever you hear a word from my mouth, you shall give them warning from me. [8]If I say to the wicked, O wicked one, you shall surely die, and you do not speak to warn the wicked to turn from his way, that wicked person shall die in his iniquity, but his blood I will require at your hand. [9]But if you warn the wicked to turn from his way, and he does not turn from his way, that person shall die in his iniquity, but you will have delivered your soul.	*Do we have the option to not care-front those who are sinning, especially those who claim to be part of God's people?*
Matthew 5:23 So if you are offering your gift at the altar and there remember that your brother has something against you, [24]leave your gift there before the altar and go. First be reconciled to your brother, and then come and offer your gift. [25]Come to terms quickly with your accuser while you are going with him to court, lest your accuser hand you over to the judge, and the judge to the guard, and you be put in prison. [26]Truly, I say to you, you will never get out until you have paid the last penny.	*If we remember that someone has something against us (they think we are the ones who have sinned), do we have the responsibility to initiate pursuing peace with them?*
James 5:19 My brothers, if anyone among you wanders from the truth and someone brings him back, [20]let him know that whoever brings back a sinner from his wandering will save his soul from death and will cover a multitude of sins.	*Why would anyone take the risk of trying to bring back someone wandering from the truth?*

Galatians 2:11 But when Cephas came to Antioch, I opposed him to his face, because he stood condemned. [12]For before certain men came from James, he was eating with the Gentiles; but when they came he drew back and separated himself, fearing the circumcision party. [13]And the rest of the Jews acted hypocritically along with him, so that even Barnabas was led astray by their hypocrisy. [14]But when I saw that their conduct was not in step with the truth of the gospel, I said to Cephas before them all, "If you, though a Jew, live like a Gentile and not like a Jew, how can you force the Gentiles to live like Jews?"	*Based on this example, are we obligated to care-front sin in even well-respected, major leaders?*
Matthew 18:15 "If your brother sins against you, go and tell him his fault, between you and him alone. If he listens to you, you have gained your brother. [16]But if he does not listen, take one or two others along with you, that every charge may be established by the evidence of two or three witnesses. [17]If he refuses to listen to them, tell it to the church. And if he refuses to listen even to the church, let him be to you as a Gentile and a tax collector. [18]Truly, I say to you, whatever you bind on earth shall be bound in heaven, and whatever you loose on earth shall be loosed in heaven. [19]Again I say to you, if two of you agree on earth about anything they ask, it will be done for them by my Father in heaven. [20]For where two or three are gathered in my name, there am I among them."	*To what extent must we pursue peace when our fellow Christian sins against us?* *Must we be willing to escalate the care-fronting?* *What authority does the local assembly of believers have in these conflict matters?*
Proverbs 25:9 Argue your case with your neighbor himself, and do not reveal another's secret, [10]lest he who hears you bring shame upon you, and your ill repute have no end.	*How does this proverb compare to Jesus' instructions in Matthew 18:15-17?*

Galatians 6:1 Brothers, if anyone is caught in any transgression, you who are spiritual should restore him in a spirit of gentleness. Keep watch on yourself, lest you too be tempted. [2]Bear one another's burdens, and so fulfill the law of Christ. [3]For if anyone thinks he is something, when he is nothing, he deceives himself. [4]But let each one test his own work, and then his reason to boast will be in himself alone and not in his neighbor. [5]For each will have to bear his own load.	*How are we to pursue a brother or sister in Christ who is caught in sin?*
Psalms 28:3 Do not drag me off with the wicked, with the workers of evil, who speak peace with their neighbors while evil is in their hearts. [4]Give to them according to their work and according to the evil of their deeds; give to them according to the work of their hands; render them their due reward.	*Can someone say they are for peace but then not work for it, revealing that they have lost the Judgment of Charity?*
Isaiah 19:2 And I will stir up Egyptians against Egyptians, and they will fight, each against another and each against his neighbor, city against city, kingdom against kingdom; [3]and the spirit of the Egyptians within them will be emptied out, and I will confound their counsel; and they will inquire of the idols and the sorcerers, and the mediums and the necromancers;	*God sends confusion and conflict on His enemies. How can unresolved conflict be part of God's judgment?*
2 Timothy 2:23 Have nothing to do with foolish, ignorant controversies; you know that they breed quarrels. [24]And the Lord's servant must not be quarrelsome but kind to everyone, able to teach, patiently enduring evil, [25]correcting his opponents with gentleness. God may perhaps grant them repentance leading to a knowledge of the truth, [26]and they may come to their senses and escape from the snare of the devil, after being captured by him to do his will.	*What is needed to correct others with gentleness?* *What must be our ultimate hope if we are to face these conflict situations correctly?*

1 Timothy 5:1 Do not rebuke an older man but encourage him as you would a father, younger men as brothers, [2]older women as mothers, younger women as sisters, in all purity.	*Are we being told NOT to care-front others? Or, are we being told HOW to care-front?*
1 Corinthians 4:19 But I will come to you soon, if the Lord wills, and I will find out not the talk of these arrogant people but their power. [20]For the kingdom of God does not consist in talk but in power. [21]What do you wish? Shall I come to you with a rod, or with love in a spirit of gentleness?	*Paul promises to care-front the situation when he comes. What evidence do you see of his willingness to speak the truth firmly? To be gracious and gentle?*
Proverbs 25:26 Like a muddied spring or a polluted fountain is a righteous man who gives way before the wicked.	*Is giving in to sin an appropriate way to seek peace in a relationship?*
Deuteronomy 1:12 How can I bear by myself the weight and burden of you and your strife?	*Does our unresolved conflict burden others?*
Proverbs 15:18 A hot-tempered man stirs up strife, but he who is slow to anger quiets contention.	*How do our anger and temper get in the way of pursuing peace?*
Proverbs 17:14 The beginning of strife is like letting out water, so quit before the quarrel breaks out.	*Why should we deal with strife as quickly as possible?*
Proverbs 20:3 It is an honor for a man to keep aloof from strife, but every fool will be quarreling.	*Should we be known as people who are always in strife?*

Ephesians 6:15 and, as shoes for your feet, having put on the readiness given by the gospel of peace.	*The armor of God includes the readiness to share the gospel. How is the good news of Jesus a "gospel of peace?"* *What does a lack of peace between professing Christians suggest about the gospel?*
Psalms 120:6 Too long have I had my dwelling among those who hate peace. ⁷ I am for peace, but when I speak, they are for war!	*Are you for peace?*
2 Corinthians 12:20 For I fear that perhaps when I come I may find you not as I wish, and that you may find me not as you wish—that perhaps there may be quarreling, jealousy, anger, hostility, slander, gossip, conceit, and disorder. **13:11** Finally, brothers, rejoice. Aim for restoration, comfort one another, agree with one another, live in peace; and the God of love and peace will be with you. ¹²Greet one another with a holy kiss.	*Paul was dealing with a divided church. What does he fear he will find when he visits them?* *A chapter later, Paul makes clear what should be our "aim." What should we be setting our sites on?*

1 John 4:7 Beloved, let us love one another, for love is from God, and whoever loves has been born of God and knows God. ⁸Anyone who does not love does not know God, because God is love. ⁹In this the love of God was made manifest among us, that God sent his only Son into the world, so that we might live through him. ¹⁰In this is love, not that we have loved God but that he loved us and sent his Son to be the propitiation for our sins. ¹¹Beloved, if God so loved us, we also ought to love one another. ¹²No one has ever seen God; if we love one another, God abides in us and his love is perfected in us. ¹³By this we know that we abide in him and he in us, because he has given us of his Spirit. ¹⁴And we have seen and testify that the Father has sent his Son to be the Savior of the world. ¹⁵Whoever confesses that Jesus is the Son of God, God abides in him, and he in God. ¹⁶So we have come to know and to believe the love that God has for us. God is love, and whoever abides in love abides in God, and God abides in him. ¹⁷By this is love perfected with us, so that we may have confidence for the day of judgment, because as he is so also are we in this world. ¹⁸There is no fear in love, but perfect love casts out fear. For fear has to do with punishment, and whoever fears has not been perfected in love. ¹⁹We love because he first loved us. ²⁰If anyone says, "I love God," and hates his brother, he is a liar; for he who does not love his brother whom he has seen cannot love God whom he has not seen. ²¹And this commandment we have from him: whoever loves God must also love his brother.

How does this extended passage by "the beloved disciple," John, address the question of the connection between our relationship with God and with other believers?

What are the requirements for God to abide in us and have His love perfected in us (note that the pronouns in verse 12 are plural)?

NOTES ON ADDITIONAL RELATED SCRIPTURAL REFERENCES:

☐ *Do I believe that I am mandated by Jesus to be an initiator in pursuing peace, especially in my relationships with other believers?*

ESCALATE WITH OTHERS

Biblical peacemakers so yearn for peace in their relationships that they not only pursue peace, they are willing to escalate the care-fronting with the help of others. The following biblical texts give support to this core commitment we must make. Review the texts and jot your notes to the answers to the questions. At the end of the study, there is a place to capture your notes on additional texts that come to mind.

Matthew 18:15 "If your brother sins against you, go and tell him his fault, between you and him alone. If he listens to you, you have gained your brother. [16]But if he does not listen, take one or two others along with you, that every charge may be established by the evidence of two or three witnesses. [17]If he refuses to listen to them, tell it to the church. And if he refuses to listen even to the church, let him be to you as a Gentile and a tax collector. [18]Truly, I say to you, whatever you bind on earth shall be bound in heaven, and whatever you loose on earth shall be loosed in heaven. [19]Again I say to you, if two of you agree on earth about anything they ask, it will be done for them by my Father in heaven. [20]For where two or three are gathered in my name, there am I among them." *(This text was also reviewed under "Pursue Peace: Biblical Foundations." This is a central passage of Jesus' specific, direct teaching on dealing with conflict.)*	*Does Jesus make it clear that we must not only go by ourselves, but we must be willing to get help from other Christians, so we can seek to reconcile the relationship?*
1 Timothy 5:19 Do not admit a charge against an elder except on the evidence of two or three witnesses. [20]As for those who persist in sin, rebuke them in the presence of all, so that the rest may stand in fear. [21]In the presence of God and of Christ Jesus and of the elect angels I charge you to keep these rules without prejudging, doing nothing from partiality.	*How do the steps of escalating care-fronting, when dealing with an elder in a local church compare with the general pattern of Matthew 18:15-17?*

Leviticus 26:14-39 *(This deals with God's escalating care-fronting His people for their sin. Please read this in your Bibles.)*	*This extended passage shows us how God escalates care-fronting His people with their sin. What principles can we gather for our escalating of conflict?*
Philippians 4:2 I entreat Euodia and I entreat Syntyche to agree in the Lord. ³Yes, I ask you also, true companion, help these women, who have labored side by side with me in the gospel together with Clement and the rest of my fellow workers, whose names are in the book of life.	*Conflict many times becomes public. Often the help of others is needed. How does Paul speak the truth in love to these women in this passage?*
1 Corinthians 6:1 When one of you has a grievance against another, does he dare go to law before the unrighteous instead of the saints? ²Or do you not know that the saints will judge the world? And if the world is to be judged by you, are you incompetent to try trivial cases? ³Do you not know that we are to judge angels? How much more, then, matters pertaining to this life! ⁴So if you have such cases, why do you lay them before those who have no standing in the church? ⁵I say this to your shame. Can it be that there is no one among you wise enough to settle a dispute between the brothers, ⁶but brother goes to law against brother, and that before unbelievers? ⁷To have lawsuits at all with one another is already a defeat for you. Why not rather suffer wrong? Why not rather be defrauded? ⁸But you yourselves wrong and defraud—even your own brothers!	*Why do you think most of us have never heard of even one time when these verses have been applied to conflict situations between professing Christians?* *What must be our posture to submit ourselves to the binding arbitration of other believers?*
Proverbs 18:17 The one who states his case first seems right, until the other comes and examines him. ¹⁸The lot puts an end to quarrels and decides between powerful contenders. ¹⁹A brother offended is more unyielding than a strong city, and quarreling is like the bars of a castle.	*Is part of escalating a conflict as a mediator to listen to all sides of the story?* *Why would folks allow a decision to be made by "lot" (like the drawing of straws) rather than give in to the desires of the other?*

Proverbs 12:15 The way of a fool is right in his own eyes, but a wise man listens to advice.	*If we will not be open to the help of others in conflict, what are we?*
Proverbs 13:10 By insolence comes nothing but strife, but with those who take advice is wisdom.	*Will an insolence, independent, prideful attitude, allow us to ask others for help or take their advice when it is given?*
Proverbs 18:1 Whoever isolates himself seeks his own desire; he breaks out against all sound judgment. ²A fool takes no pleasure in understanding, but only in expressing his opinion.	*Conflict tends to make us stop listening and start blaming. If someone isolates himself from the help of others, what are they seeking?*
Proverbs 15:12 A scoffer does not like to be reproved; he will not go to the wise.	*Why will the scoffer not initiate going to the wise?*
2 Corinthians 2:4 "For I wrote to you out of much affliction and anguish of heart and with many tears, not to cause you pain but to let you know the abundant love that I have for you."	*Can dealing with conflict be gut-wrenching, even for apostles?* *What was Paul's motivation that helped him push through that pain?*

NOTES ON ADDITIONAL RELATED SCRIPTURAL REFERENCES:

☐ *Do I believe that my pursuit of peace is so important that I will go through the pain of escalating it, even when it means asking others to help me?*

ACQUIRE THE JUDGMENT OF CHARITY

Here we look over some of the biblical texts that help us become convinced that the commitment to acquire the Judgment of Charity is core to becoming a peacemaker. We will see that only God can truly know another person's motives. Even our self-understanding is easily distorted, though we usually give ourselves the Judgment of Charity. When it comes to others, we can slip into being judgmental and allowing anger and hurt to rule how we face conflict. At the end of this section, there is a place to note other passages the Lord may bring to your mind.

2 Corinthians 5:16 From now on, therefore, we regard no one according to the flesh. Even though we once regarded Christ according to the flesh, we regard him thus no longer. ¹⁷Therefore, if anyone is in Christ, he is a new creation. The old has passed away; behold, the new has come.	*To regard others "according to the flesh" is to look merely at external methods. What is included in the Judgment of Charity toward fellow-believers?*
1 Kings 8:39 . . . then hear in heaven your dwelling place and forgive and act and render to each whose heart you know, according to all his ways (for you, you only, know the hearts of all the children of mankind), ⁴⁰that they may fear you all the days that they live in the land that you gave to our fathers.	*Who is the only One Who knows the hearts of people? Are we in a position to be the judge of others' motives?*
1 Corinthians 4:3 But with me it is a very small thing that I should be judged by you or by any human court. In fact, I do not even judge myself. ⁴For I am not aware of anything against myself, but I am not thereby acquitted. It is the Lord who judges me. ⁵Therefore do not pronounce judgment before the time, before the Lord comes, who will bring to light the things now hidden in darkness and will disclose the purposes of the heart. Then each one will receive his commendation from God.	*Why shouldn't we put ourselves in the position to judge others' motives?* *Can we be certain about our own motives, even if we have a clear conscience?* *When will the purposes of our hearts be revealed?*

Proverbs 21:2 Every way of a man is right in his own eyes, but the Lord weighs the heart.	*Do we give ourselves the Judgment of Charity?*
1 Corinthians 2:11 For who knows a person's thoughts except the spirit of that person, which is in him? So also no one comprehends the thoughts of God except the Spirit of God.	*Can we read other people's minds?* *Can we know for certain what another person's motives are?*
Proverbs 16:2 All the ways of a man are pure in his own eyes, but the Lord weighs the spirit.	*By default, do we give ourselves the Judgment of Charity?*
Hebrews 4:12 For the word of God is living and active, sharper than any two-edged sword, piercing to the division of soul and of spirit, of joints and of marrow, and discerning the thoughts and intentions of the heart. ¹³And no creature is hidden from his sight, but all are naked and exposed to the eyes of him to whom we must give account.	*We tend to give ourselves the Judgment of Charity. What does God use to help us see what's really happening within us?*
Psalm 19:12 Who can discern his errors? Declare me innocent from hidden faults. ¹³Keep back your servant also from presumptuous sins; let them not have dominion over me! Then I shall be blameless, and innocent of great transgression. ¹⁴Let the words of my mouth and the meditation of my heart be acceptable in your sight, O Lord, my rock and my redeemer.	*How can an understanding of how easily we fool ourselves help us to have a spirit of humility when it comes to conflict situations?* *Do we need God's help to see our own faults?*
Jeremiah 17:9 The heart is deceitful above all things, and desperately sick; who can understand it? ¹⁰"I the Lord search the heart and test the mind, to give every man according to his ways, according to the fruit of his deeds."	*Our sinfulness deceives us. Who knows our motives? Who holds us accountable for our deeds?*

Matthew 7:1 "Judge not, that you be not judged. [2]For with the judgment you pronounce you will be judged, and with the measure you use it will be measured to you. [3]Why do you see the speck that is in your brother's eye, but do not notice the log that is in your own eye? [4]Or how can you say to your brother, 'Let me take the speck out of your eye,' when there is the log in your own eye? [5]You hypocrite, first take the log out of your own eye, and then you will see clearly to take the speck out of your brother's eye. [6]"Do not give dogs what is holy, and do not throw your pearls before pigs, lest they trample them underfoot and turn to attack you.	*We must all make judgment calls. Like who are the "dogs" in verse 6. But we do not need to be judgmental. How does "the measure we use" reflect if we have lost the Judgment of Charity?* *Why is it critical to look within ourselves first, before correcting others?*
Romans 14:13 Therefore let us not pass judgment on one another any longer, but rather decide never to put a stumbling block or hindrance in the way of a brother.	*In dealing with disputable matters, should we judge another's motives?*
James 4:11 Do not speak evil against one another, brothers. The one who speaks against a brother or judges his brother, speaks evil against the law and judges the law. But if you judge the law, you are not a doer of the law but a judge. [12]There is only one lawgiver and judge, he who is able to save and to destroy. But who are you to judge your neighbor?	*Whose position do we take when we posture ourselves to be a judge, especially of others' motives?*
James 2:1 My brothers, show no partiality as you hold the faith in our Lord Jesus Christ, the Lord of glory. [2]For if a man wearing a gold ring and fine clothing comes into your assembly, and a poor man in shabby clothing also comes in, [3]and if you pay attention to the one who wears the fine clothing and say, "You sit here in a good place," while you say to the poor man, "You stand over there," or, "Sit down at my feet," [4]have you not then made distinctions among yourselves and become judges with evil thoughts?	*"Judges with evil thoughts" show partiality. How does this show up in conflict situations?*

James 2:12 So speak and so act as those who are to be judged under the law of liberty. ¹³For judgment is without mercy to one who has shown no mercy. Mercy triumphs over judgment.	*How should a Christian's experience of mercy impact her efforts to acquire the Judgment of Charity?*
James 3:13 Who is wise and understanding among you? By his good conduct let him show his works in the meekness of wisdom. ¹⁴But if you have bitter jealousy and selfish ambition in your hearts, do not boast and be false to the truth. ¹⁵This is not the wisdom that comes down from above, but is earthly, unspiritual, demonic. ¹⁶For where jealousy and selfish ambition exist, there will be disorder and every vile practice. ¹⁷But the wisdom from above is first pure, then peaceable, gentle, open to reason, full of mercy and good fruits, impartial and sincere. ¹⁸And a harvest of righteousness is sown in peace by those who make peace.	*How is the Judgment of Charity an expression of "wisdom from above?"* *How is the judgment of bitterness an expression of wisdom from below?*
James 5:9 Do not grumble against one another, brothers, so that you may not be judged; behold, the Judge is standing at the door.	*How does grumbling, often against each other's motives, reflect that we have taken God's seat as Judge?*
Luke 6:37 Judge not, and you will not be judged; condemn not, and you will not be condemned; forgive, and you will be forgiven; ³⁸give, and it will be given to you. Good measure, pressed down, shaken together, running over, will be put into your lap. For with the measure you use it will be measured back to you.	*Why is it beneficial for us to acquire the Judgment of Charity toward others, using the super-sized measure of grace?*
1 Samuel 26:25 Then Saul said to David, "Blessed be you, my son David! You will do many things and will succeed in them." So David went his way, and Saul returned to his place. ²⁷:¹Then David said in his heart, "Now I shall perish one day by the hand of Saul. There is nothing better for me than that I should escape to the land of the Philistines. Then Saul will despair of seeking me any longer within the borders of Israel, and I shall escape out of his hand."	*King Saul said that David's refusal to kill him when he had the chance proved to him what David's motives were. Yet, do the opening verses of chapter 27 indicate that Saul's Judgment of Charity was restored toward David?*

1 Chronicles 19:2 And David said, "I will deal kindly with Hanun the son of Nahash, for his father dealt kindly with me." So David sent messengers to console him concerning his father. And David's servants came to the land of the Ammonites to Hanun to console him. ³But the princes of the Ammonites said to Hanun, "Do you think, because David has sent comforters to you, that he is honoring your father? Have not his servants come to you to search and to overthrow and to spy out the land?"	*Other people can sometimes cause us to doubt the motives of others. What impact can this have on our Judgment of Charity toward them?*
James 1:19 Know this, my beloved brothers: let every person be quick to hear, slow to speak, slow to anger; ²⁰for the anger of man does not produce the righteousness of God.	*How are these action steps, especially in a conflict situation, a reflection of seeking the Judgment of Charity?*
Ephesians 4:26 Be angry and do not sin; do not let the sun go down on your anger, ²⁷and give no opportunity to the devil.	*How quickly can we lose the Judgment of Charity amid conflict?*
Psalm 62:3 How long will all of you attack a man to batter him, like a leaning wall, a tottering fence? ⁴They only plan to thrust him down from his high position. They take pleasure in falsehood. They bless with their mouths, but inwardly they curse.	*What does it feel like to continue to have our motives judged negatively, talking peace with us but running us down to others?*
Proverbs 20:22 Do not say, "I will repay evil"; wait for the Lord, and he will deliver you.	*Acquiring the Judgment of Charity includes entrusting final judgment to God. How does this verse relate to Romans 12:17-21?*

Proverbs 14:29 Whoever is slow to anger has great understanding, but he who has a hasty temper exalts folly.	*What is the relationship between the Judgment of Charity and being slow to anger?*
Proverbs 15:1 A soft answer turns away wrath, but a harsh word stirs up anger.	*As we acquire the Judgment of Charity, our responses tend to become "softer." Why is this so important?*
Proverbs 15:28 The heart of the righteous ponders how to answer, but the mouth of the wicked pours out evil things.	*How does seeking the Judgment of Charity help the righteous ponder how to answer?*
James 4:1 What causes quarrels and what causes fights among you? Is it not this, that your passions are at war within you? ²You desire and do not have, so you murder. You covet and cannot obtain, so you fight and quarrel. You do not have, because you do not ask. ³You ask and do not receive, because you ask wrongly, to spend it on your passions.	*Why is it so important to realize the nature of the spiritual battles that lie behind quarrels?*
2 Corinthians 6:11 We have spoken freely to you, Corinthians; our heart is wide open. ¹²You are not restricted by us, but you are restricted in your own affections. ¹³In return (I speak as to children) widen your hearts also.	*Does it seem like the Apostle Paul thought that some of the people in Corinth had lost the Judgment of Charity toward him?*

NOTES ON ADDITIONAL RELATED SCRIPTURAL REFERENCES:

☐ *Do I believe that I am to pursue peace, not just working through the methods in the conflict, but all the way to the heart of the matter, seeking the restoration of the Judgment of Charity?*

CHOOSE TRUE FORGIVENESS

The Judgment of Charity is essential to long-term, meaningful relationships of peace. But, we all have sinned and have been sinned against. It will happen again in the future. So, how can we restore the Judgment of Charity? The answer is through forgiveness. The following passages help us explore why this commitment is expected of the Christ-follower. At the end of the section, there is a place for you to capture additional applicable texts that the Holy Spirit brings to your mind.

Luke 7:40 And Jesus answering said to him, "Simon, I have something to say to you." And he answered, "Say it, Teacher." [41]"A certain moneylender had two debtors. One owed five hundred denarii, and the other fifty. [42]When they could not pay, he cancelled the debt of both. Now which of them will love him more?" [43]Simon answered, "The one, I suppose, for whom he cancelled the larger debt." And he said to him, "You have judged rightly." [44]Then turning toward the woman he said to Simon, "Do you see this woman? I entered your house; you gave me no water for my feet, but she has wet my feet with her tears and wiped them with her hair. [45]You gave me no kiss, but from the time I came in she has not ceased to kiss my feet. [46]You did not anoint my head with oil, but she has anointed my feet with ointment. [47]Therefore I tell you, her sins, which are many, are forgiven—for she loved much. But he who is forgiven little, loves little."	*How does our understanding about how much we have been forgiven of by God impact the way we love Him?* *Can it also have an impact on how we forgive others?*
Luke 23:32 Two others, who were criminals, were led away to be put to death with him. [33]And when they came to the place that is called The Skull, there they crucified him, and the criminals, one on his right and one on his left. [34]And Jesus said, "Father, forgive them, for they know not what they do." And they cast lots to divide his garments.	*How is Jesus a model for us, as He hung on the cross?*

Genesis 50:17 'Say to Joseph, "Please forgive the transgression of your brothers and their sin, because they did evil to you."' And now, please forgive the transgression of the servants of the God of your father." Joseph wept when they spoke to him. [18]His brothers also came and fell down before him and said, "Behold, we are your servants." [19]But Joseph said to them, "Do not fear, for am I in the place of God? [20]As for you, you meant evil against me, but God meant it for good, to bring it about that many people should be kept alive, as they are today. [21]So do not fear; I will provide for you and your little ones." Thus he comforted them and spoke kindly to them.	*How does Joseph model for us the need for faith in God when forgiving others?*
Proverbs 19:11 Good sense makes one slow to anger, and it is his [the king's] glory to overlook an offense.	*Why is it to the king's glory to overlook an offense?*
Ephesians 4:29 Let no corrupting talk come out of your mouths, but only such as is good for building up, as fits the occasion, that it may give grace to those who hear. [30]And do not grieve the Holy Spirit of God, by whom you were sealed for the day of redemption. [31]Let all bitterness and wrath and anger and clamor and slander be put away from you, along with all malice. [32]Be kind to one another, tenderhearted, forgiving one another, as God in Christ forgave you.	*How does relational discord, especially between Christians, grieve the Holy Spirit?* *What is the relationship between having the Judgment of Charity and being "tenderhearted?"* *What is the standard by which we should forgive others?*

Matthew 6:11 Give us this day our daily bread, [12]and forgive us our debts, as we also have forgiven our debtors. [13]And lead us not into temptation, but deliver us from evil. [14]For if you forgive others their trespasses, your heavenly Father will also forgive you, [15]but if you do not forgive others their trespasses, neither will your Father forgive your trespasses.	*Why is our forgiveness of others so important?* *We do not earn God's forgiveness, even by our forgiving of others. Rather, what does our unwillingness to forgive tell us about our relationship with God?*
Matthew 18:21 Then Peter came up and said to him, "Lord, how often will my brother sin against me, and I forgive him? As many as seven times?" [22]Jesus said to him, "I do not say to you seven times, but seventy-seven times." (*See the rest of the parable in verses 23-31*) [32]"Then his master summoned him and said to him, 'You wicked servant! I forgave you all that debt because you pleaded with me. [33]And should not you have had mercy on your fellow servant, as I had mercy on you?' [34]And in anger his master delivered him to the jailers, until he should pay all his debt. [35]So also my heavenly Father will do to every one of you, if you do not forgive your brother from your heart."	*Jesus standard for our extending forgiveness is impossible without His help. How does this parable expand on the commandment of Ephesians 4:32 to forgive as we have been forgiven?*
Proverbs 17:9 Whoever covers an offense seeks love, but he who repeats a matter separates close friends.	*When God forgave us in Christ, He covered our sin with Jesus' blood. Why is the "covering" of past sins essential for maintaining a close friendship?*
1 Peter 4:8 Above all, keep loving one another earnestly, since love covers a multitude of sins. [9]Show hospitality to one another without grumbling.	*If we say that we love other believers, must we also be willing to forgive them?*

Exodus 34:6 The Lord passed before him and proclaimed, "The Lord, the Lord, a God merciful and gracious, slow to anger, and abounding in steadfast love and faithfulness, [7]keeping steadfast love for thousands, forgiving iniquity and transgression and sin, but who will by no means clear the guilty, visiting the iniquity of the fathers on the children and the children's children, to the third and the fourth generation."	*How is God's character a perfect model of covenant-faithful love and forgiveness AND expecting the accountability of changed lives?*
Amos 1:11 Thus says the Lord: "For three transgressions of Edom, and for four, I will not revoke the punishment, because he pursued his brother with the sword and cast off all pity, and his anger tore perpetually, and he kept his wrath forever.	*What was the sin of Edom that God said He was going to punish?* *What is the evidence that these people lost the Judgment of Charity toward the people of Israel?*

NOTES ON ADDITIONAL RELATED SCRIPTURAL REFERENCES:

☐ *Do I believe that biblical forgiveness is essential to the restoration of the Judgment of Charity, which is needful in the pursuit of the peace of reconciliation?*

EXPECT ACCOUNTABILITY

Missing from many popular discussions of conflict resolution and forgiveness is the concept of accountability. This includes the importance of repentance and the resulting manifestation of the fruits of repentance. We must expect ourselves and others to be held accountable for our methods. This accountability includes the authority of the local church assembly to judge in extending forgiveness and withholding it. The following are some biblical texts that teach us that God expects accountability and that He wants us to do so as well. There is room at the end to add notes on other texts that the Lord may bring to your mind regarding this core commitment.

Deuteronomy 29:18 Beware lest there be among you a man or woman or clan or tribe whose heart is turning away today from the Lord our God to go and serve the gods of those nations. Beware lest there be among you a root bearing poisonous and bitter fruit, ¹⁹one who, when he hears the words of this sworn covenant, blesses himself in his heart, saying, 'I shall be safe, though I walk in the stubbornness of my heart.' This will lead to the sweeping away of moist and dry alike. ²⁰The Lord will not be willing to forgive him, but rather the anger of the Lord and his jealousy will smoke against that man, and the curses written in this book will settle upon him, and the Lord will blot out his name from under heaven.	*Why is it so dangerous to assume that God does not know the intentions of our hearts?* *Why would the LORD not be willing to forgive?*
2 Chronicles 7:13 When I shut up the heavens so that there is no rain, or command the locust to devour the land, or send pestilence among my people, ¹⁴if my people who are called by my name humble themselves and pray and seek my face and turn from their wicked ways, then I will hear from heaven and will forgive their sin and heal their land.	*God offers to forgive. What are the requirements to receive His forgiveness? Is repentance one of those?*

1 Corinthians 5:1 It is actually reported that there is sexual immorality among you, and of a kind that is not tolerated even among pagans, for a man has his father's wife. ²And you are arrogant! Ought you not rather to mourn? Let him who has done this be removed from among you.

³For though absent in body, I am present in spirit; and as if present, I have already pronounced judgment on the one who did such a thing. ⁴When you are assembled in the name of the Lord Jesus and my spirit is present, with the power of our Lord Jesus, ⁵you are to deliver this man to Satan for the destruction of the flesh, so that his spirit may be saved in the day of the Lord.

⁶Your boasting is not good. Do you not know that a little leaven leavens the whole lump? ⁷Cleanse out the old leaven that you may be a new lump, as you really are unleavened. For Christ, our Passover lamb, has been sacrificed. ⁸Let us therefore celebrate the festival, not with the old leaven, the leaven of malice and evil, but with the unleavened bread of sincerity and truth.

⁹I wrote to you in my letter not to associate with sexually immoral people— ¹⁰not at all meaning the sexually immoral of this world, or the greedy and swindlers, or idolaters, since then you would need to go out of the world. ¹¹But now I am writing to you not to associate with anyone who bears the name of brother if he is guilty of sexual immorality or greed, or is an idolater, reviler, drunkard, or swindler—not even to eat with such a one. ¹²For what have I to do with judging outsiders? Is it not those inside the church whom you are to judge? ¹³God judges those outside. "Purge the evil person from among you."

This extended passage helps us see the Apostle Paul's commitment to expect accountability. When the Corinthian church did not church-discipline this man, was it out of love or out of arrogance?

Several times Paul mentions pronouncing judgment (v. 3) and our responsibility to judge those who claim to be Christians within the local church (v. 12). How does this not violate the teaching of Jesus NOT to judge?

2 Corinthians 2:5 Now if anyone has caused pain, he has caused it not to me, but in some measure—not to put it too severely—to all of you. [6]For such a one, this punishment by the majority is enough, [7]so you should rather turn to forgive and comfort him, or he may be overwhelmed by excessive sorrow. [8]So I beg you to reaffirm your love for him. [9]For this is why I wrote, that I might test you and know whether you are obedient in everything. [10]Anyone whom you forgive, I also forgive. Indeed, what I have forgiven, if I have forgiven anything, has been for your sake in the presence of Christ, [11]so that we would not be outwitted by Satan; for we are not ignorant of his designs.	*We do not know if this repentant person is the same man as mentioned in 1 Corinthians, but this passage does help us understand what we should do if someone has repented.* *If we will not forgive and comfort, what could happen to the penitent person?* *What could happen to the local body of Christ?*
2 Corinthians 7:9 As it is, I rejoice, not because you were grieved, but because you were grieved into repenting. For you felt a godly grief, so that you suffered no loss through us. [10]For godly grief produces a repentance that leads to salvation without regret, whereas worldly grief produces death. [11]For see what earnestness this godly grief has produced in you, but also what eagerness to clear yourselves, what indignation, what fear, what longing, what zeal, what punishment! At every point you have proved yourselves innocent in the matter.	*The Apostle Paul expected accountability. He was willing to care-front, even though it was hard. What is the good result of his caring enough to confront?*
Luke 17:3 Pay attention to yourselves! If your brother sins, rebuke him, and if he repents, forgive him, [4]and if he sins against you seven times in the day, and turns to you seven times, saying, 'I repent,' you must forgive him."	*Are we to initiate care-fronting when we see another Christian sinning?* *How often must we extend forgiveness?* *Are we expected to act like forgiveness is complete, that there is now reconciliation, IF there has not been an expression of repentance?*

Proverbs 26:20 For lack of wood the fire goes out, and where there is no whisperer, quarreling ceases. ²¹As charcoal to hot embers and wood to fire, so is a quarrelsome man for kindling strife. ²²The words of a whisperer are like delicious morsels; they go down into the inner parts of the body.	*The "whisperer" is a gossip. A quarrelsome person kindles strife, often by sharing bad things behind someone's back for no good purpose. Does a gossiper give others the Judgment of Charity?*
Titus 3:10 As for a person who stirs up division, after warning him once and then twice, have nothing more to do with him, ¹¹knowing that such a person is warped and sinful; he is self-condemned.	*Is divisiveness a sin worthy of church discipline?*
John 20:21 Jesus said to them again, "Peace be with you. As the Father has sent me, even so I am sending you." ²²And when he had said this, he breathed on them and said to them, "Receive the Holy Spirit. ²³If you forgive the sins of any, they are forgiven them; if you withhold forgiveness from any, it is withheld."	*Does Jesus give us some measure of authority when it comes to forgiveness?* *From whom would we withhold forgiveness? Why?*

NOTES ON ADDITIONAL RELATED SCRIPTURAL REFERENCES:

☐ *Do I believe that people should be held accountable to manifest the fruits of repentance in the future, but that my forgiveness of their past sins is tied to their declaration of repentance?*

ONE-PAGE TRAINING SHEETS

One-page training sheets attempt to boil down the key concepts and tools needed to pursue peace biblically. While there are some topics that carry over to two pages, the goal was to keep things concise.

The "sidebar box" at the top of each sheet has a brief definition or description.

The main portion of the page fills in more details and examples.

The Pop Quiz is a challenge to make sure that you can think through and communicate the key concept.

"So then let us pursue what makes for peace and for mutual upbuilding."

Romans 14:19

JUDGMENT OF CHARITY

The **decision of the will** to actively think from God's perspective regarding another person's motives.

It is the **active choice** to seek a verdict regarding another person's motives in the court of God's love.

We give someone the judgment of love, rather than bitterness, when **we assume the best possible motives** for the other person's methods.

The Judgment of Charity is a phrase used by the Puritans. William Perkins certainly advocates fighting for the Judgment of Charity when he said, *"Despise not thy neighbour, but think thyself as bad a sinner, and that the like defects may befall thee. If thou canst not excuse his doing, excuse his intent which may be good; or if the deed be evil, think it was done of ignorance; if thou canst no way excuse him, think some great temptation befell him, and that thou shouldest be worse if the like temptation befell thee; and give God thanks that the like as yet hath not befallen thee. Despise not a man being a sinner, for though he be evil today, he may turn tomorrow."*

Jesus tells us not to judge, lest we be judged. He does not mean that we never have to make judgments. Matthew 7 also says Jesus does not want us to give dogs what is holy. We must make a judgment about who is a "dog." Jesus is telling us not to be judgmental. This becomes clear in verse 2 where we are told that the measure we use on others will be used on us. If we want others to measure out the judgment of love toward our motives, we too must use the same super-sized scoop of grace towards theirs.

This practical outworking of love is based on the confident assurance that God will ultimately judge the thoughts and intentions of <u>all</u> our hearts. We can trust that He will do right at the right time.

The Judgment of Charity is an answer to the question, "How?" *How* can I open my friend's filters so that they can really hear me? *How* can I listen better and really seek to understand the other person? *How* can I speak the truth in love? *How* can I melt someone's hard shell so that we can really put everything on the table? *How* can I forgive them after what they did to me?

Knowing that only God can fully understand someone else's intentions, we transform our thinking (and in turn, our feelings) about others. We regard others for who they are in Christ and not primarily by their actions. At least, we seek to regard others for who they could be in Christ. Thus, the Judgment of Charity even applies to our enemies. With this transformed perspective, we choose to seek their good as fellow members of the family of Christ, or as those in the world whom God loves.

> **POP QUIZ:**
>
> Does the Judgment of Charity mean that we don't hold others responsible for their methods?

JUDGMENT OF CHARITY VERSUS THE BENEFIT OF THE DOUBT

The "Benefit of the Doubt" is the **weaker cousin** of the "Judgment of Charity." It tends to refrain from assuming the worst motives behind the other person's methods.

The Judgment of Charity fights to assume the best possible motives that could lie behind another's actions.

Some will incorrectly assume that the Judgment of Charity is the same as what is commonly referred to as the "benefit of the doubt." This is too negative a phrase to express the strength of the resources available to Christ-followers. We know that our heavenly Father is on the throne and that He is the righteous Judge to Whom we can entrust our situation. We have confidence that our identity is secure in Christ, so we don't have to posture ourselves defensively. We have the Holy Spirit Who will help us fulfill our calling as witnesses of Christ's reconciling work.

When we give "the benefit," we don't allow ourselves to impute horrible motives to the other person. The Judgment of Charity seeks to assume the best possible intentions behind someone's actions. We actively posture ourselves as heralds of the Good News of Jesus, rather than as judges.

The difference is comparable to the world's understanding of the "Golden Rule." Many will say that we shouldn't do to others what we don't what them to do to us. That is not what Jesus taught us. We are to *actively* do unto others what we wish them to do to us. The Judgment of Charity is an active choice, not a passive one.

Focusing on the best possible motives may include showing grace because another person may have been deceived by sin or the devil. It may be that their motives are driven by hurts from their past. It does not mean that we assume that another person's motives are always "good" or "right" in themselves.

POP QUIZ:

Why is the Judgment of Charity more difficult for non-believers to give to others?

E.L.M.

The three steps that we take to fight for the Judgment of Charity form the acronym of ELM. They picture lowering a tree, as a bridge over a raging river. They make possible a way for reconciliation.

- **Entrust** ultimate judgment of another's motives to God.

- **Lower** our own self-centered defenses.

- **Make a way** forward possible by assuming the best possible motives for the other person's methods.

We must ENTRUST ultimate judgment of motives to God, knowing that He knows the beginning from the end. This includes giving over to Him the assessment of our own motives, since we are not able to be a fair judge of even them. As we take this action step, we find ourselves resting in God's powerful position as the Judge of the universe.

We LOWER our self-centered defenses. Corresponding to the negative descriptions given in 1 Corinthians 13, we stop seeking to defend ourselves or assert ourselves. Rather, having great confidence in God's protection, we make ourselves vulnerable. We no longer have to boil with envy or brag, puffing up our own importance. Our ill-manners, that put others off, suddenly have no place. Seeking our own interests, being so touchy that we are easily angered, along with adding up an accounting of wrongs done to us — these all fall away from our field of view. The wall, that we hide behind and peek out from in order to hurl attacks, is torn down. By an act of our wills, trusting God for safety, we move from seeking the interests of ourselves to the interests of "us."

Love MAKES A WAY for truth, and for relationships to be strengthened and restored. We MAKE A WAY by choosing to assume the best motives possible, or at least the most excusable ones imaginable, on the part of others. We do this to create a path that will allow for us to reach and be reached by the other.

This is like God, in that He initiated and made a way for us to be brought back into relationship with Him. He did not take away our choice to cross the bridge, but He did go first and drop the bridge over the gorge. Yet, we must choose to cross it. He does not pretend all have crossed the bridge and that all are reconciled to Him. Nor do we live with the naivety that imagines that the presence of a bridge is the sure indicator of a unified relationship. But we know that, as apprentices of Jesus, we too must lay down the bridge of restoration and reconciliation.

POP QUIZ:

Do our efforts at building a bridge mean that reconciliation is automatically present?

CARE-FRONTING

David Augsburger's term for **caring enough to confront.** It tends to be received as less adversarial that the raw term, "confront."

David Augsburger introduced this helpful term, a combination of "caring + confronting." Many of us are hesitant to engage in seeking a resolution to our conflicts because we do not want to see people get hurt. We hear the instruction to "confront" and all we can imagine are angry tones, raised voices, deadly silence, and everyone fighting to prove their own case.

Augsburger's term reminds us that we confront relational challenges because we care enough to do so. Yes, it may be scary and perhaps things will get worse. But, we care enough to have a real, meaningful relationship with the other party that we work past these fears. We care too much to allow the wall that has been built up between us to grow any firmer or higher.

When should we care-front? Some will suggest that we should just bear up with one another. The Bible does teach us that. But, when do we stop bearing up and care-front? Honesty seems to be the critical component at this point of decision. We can bear up until we cannot bear up anymore. We must be honest with ourselves, asking the Holy Spirit to help us. Once we sense a wall going up that separates us from the other party and when we feel the freedom of the relationship strain under the tension, we are mandated to pursue peace by TRI'ing (Taking Responsibility & Initiative) to care-front.

POP QUIZ:

"Why is it NOT caring to NOT confront when we sense a wall between us and others?"

1 CORINTHIANS 13 LOVE

"Charity" is the old English word for "love." Christians are commanded to do ALL in love (see 1 Corinthians 16:14). These are practical definitions of love's motives and methods.

Love "bears all things, believes all things, hopes all things, and endures all things." The Judgment of Charity chooses to *bear up* with the irritating habits of others. It decides to *believe* that others act out of what makes sense to them. It continues to *hope* that God can change others and us, helping all to become more Christ-like. Love *endures* until Jesus comes and changes others and ourselves to become all we will be in Him. The following self-assessment can help us take the log out of our own eye first (see Matthew 7:5).

LOVE – A SELF ASSESSMENT BASED ON 1 CORINTHIANS 13 RATE YOURSELF ON THE FOLLOWING TRAITS THAT PAUL USES TO DEFINE "LOVE"						
Easily losing patience when others are "slow" in their "get-it-factor"	1	2	3	4	5	Patient and longsuffering
Gruff and stingy	1	2	3	4	5	Showing kindness through a practical, generous thoughtfulness
Boiling with envy, coveting others' success, gifts, or opportunities	1	2	3	4	5	Rejoicing and making much of the success of others
Constantly bragging about what I've accomplished and how hard I work	1	2	3	4	5	Meek and humble, willing to wash others' feet without telling people about it
Puffing up my own importance, always "padding my resume" in front of others and being easily offended when others forget to thank me	1	2	3	4	5	Seeing myself like God sees me, using what He has given me to make much of Him
Behaving shamefully, rudely butting in and demanding my way on my time schedule	1	2	3	4	5	Displaying good manners that help others feel at ease and empowered
Seeking my own interests, only serving when if fulfills me and I can have fun doing it with friends	1	2	3	4	5	Looking to the interests of others
Living with a hair-trigger, being easily angered when things don't go my way	1	2	3	4	5	Even tempered, quickly assuming the Judgment of Charity in questionable situations
Keeping a mental list of others' sins and faults, adding them up regularly so I am ready to "let them have it"	1	2	3	4	5	Forgiving others in the same way that God has forgiven me
Letting other people's idiosyncrasies get on my nerves, making me act like a bear towards them	1	2	3	4	5	Always choosing to bear up with these habits of others that tend to irritate me
Assuming the worst about others, believing in conspiracies and making a catastrophe out of most things	1	2	3	4	5	Always choosing to believe that others act out of that which makes sense to them
Convinced that people are who they are and they never really change, no matter what they say	1	2	3	4	5	Always choosing to hope that God can change others
Sprinting in relationships, starting fast but ending quickly	1	2	3	4	5	Always choosing to endure until Jesus comes and changes others (and me)
TOTAL OF EACH COLUMN						TOTAL OF EACH COLUMN
TOTAL SCORE						TOTAL SCORE
13-25 = Noisy Gong 26-39 = Still Too Much About "Me" 39-52 = Learning to Love 53-65 = Serving Excellently						

HOW WE TREAT JESUS

Jesus so identifies with His people that **how we treat Christians is how we act toward Him.** What we have done for "one of the least of these MY BROTHERS" is what we have done or left undone for Jesus.

1 John 4 says it powerfully. *"If anyone says, "I love God," and hates his brother, he is a liar; for he who does not love his brother whom he has seen cannot love God whom he has not seen. And this commandment we have from him: whoever loves God must also love his brother"* (20-21).

It is shameful. The way we treat Jesus is often with great rudeness. We puff ourselves up in arrogance and insist on our own way, even when the decision rightfully belongs to another. When we do not get our own way, we are resentful and irritable. Often, we declare our disgust by leaving, saying it a matter of sin. Yet, we do not pursue peace by escalating with the help of others. We merely put ourselves, as an individual or couple, in the position of judge and begin to treat the other like a tax-gatherer or Gentile. We separate ourselves from them.

Most of us cannot imagine being so coarse with the Savior. But, Jesus said that how we treat Christians is how we treat Him. God's standard is love. It is the most critical identifying mark of the believer. Yet, the readiness that so many have to divide the body of Christ must horrify our Lord.

Do we love Jesus? *Love . . . waits patiently, shows kindness, **does not** . . . boil with envy, brag, puff up its own importance, behave shamefully, seek its own interests, get easily-angered, add up a record of wrongs. Does not take pleasure in wrong-doing, but joyfully celebrates the truth. Always bears up, always believes, always hopes, always endures (author's translation of 1 Corinthians 13:4-7).*

POP QUIZ:

"Why is the way we treat fellow-Christians so important?"

CHANGING ME – INFLUENCING YOU

In the pursuit of peace, we must realize that we have the most control over ourselves. We cannot change others. But, we can change how we deal with the conflict and that will have the greatest chance of influencing others to change as well.

"How do I change them?!" That is often what people ask when attending a conflict mediation seminar. *"I want to know how to fix them."* This notion, that we can change other people, will often impact our methods of communication and conflict resolution, making others even more defensive and even less willing to change.

We must not take responsibility for other people's choices. But, it is critical that we take full responsibility for our own. Our behaviors, our methods, do not make others act in a certain way. Nor do their actions "force" us to respond with anger or hurt or frustration. We can choose how to respond, even to the point of loving our enemies. Other people's bad decisions do not justify our poor reactions.

Our behaviors may not control others, but they certainly influence them. The greatest impact we can have on the methods others use is to change the methods we use. This relates to the styles of conflict management we use, how we speak the truth in love, and the accountability we expect.

.

POP QUIZ:

"What can we do to have the greatest influence on changing others?"

UNDERSTANDING, NOT EXCUSING

As we pursue peace in our relationships, it is necessary for us to want to understand others. We may have witnessed their methods, but we must talk with them about their motives.

When we have been hurt, it is easy to think that seeking this understanding is the same as giving them an excuse for their hurtful behavior. Since we are responsible for our methods, even if our motives are good or understandable, we do not have to connect understanding with excusing.

Our quest to understand others' motives, communication filters, and objectives is often hindered by the fear that such knowledge will somehow provide an excuse for the hurtful behavior we have experienced. As a mediator we can remind the hurt person that we are discussing these things because perhaps the wrong methods were not motivated by malicious motives. We can point out that a person is responsible for their methods, no matter what their motives were.

This posture allows us to expect accountability for a person's methods, while showing grace and understanding for their motives. This allows us to speak the truth in love. *"While you may have been harsh to me because of your upbringing, it was still hurtful and wrong. I hear you when you say that you didn't maliciously intend to hurt me, but I need you to own responsibility for what you did."*

POP QUIZ:

"Why is a person's explanation of their motives often perceived as being self-defensive?"

CAN TRUST BE REBUILT WITHOUT THE JUDGMENT OF CHARITY?

Without love, and the judgment of love, that we have referred to as "the Judgment of Charity," it is impossible to rebuild trust.

When we do not have the Judgment of Charity, we will find ourselves being judgmental, connecting the dots of the "facts" in negative ways. Even if the mediation process has yielded specific action steps that we understand to be the fruits of repentance, our "judgment" of them will be, *"Not good enough."* Thus, the process of forgiveness will be short-circuited, and trust will never be fully restored.

Our communication filters process all the information that comes to us. If we have on blue sunglasses, everything looks blue. If yellow, then yellow. We may imagine that we are objective judges of the facts, when in reality we always wear colored glasses. The question is not whether we wear them, but which pair do we choose. Do we choose mercy-colored or judgment-colored? As James tells us, "Mercy triumphs over judgment" (James 2:13).

In my experience, when the Judgment of Charity has been lost in a marriage, there is almost nothing that can be done to repair the relationship. For even the truly repentant spouse will not be perfect. If we have on our judgment-colored glasses, we will see their slip-up as convincing proof that nothing has really changed. They really are still the problem!

With our judgment-colored glasses on, the time when trust should be rebuilding will become a time to be on the lookout for WHEN they fall. But, if we look at the repentant party through the eyes of love, we are looking for, praying for, and rooting for them to win. This allows the process of rebuilding trust to keep moving forward, even if at times it is four steps forward and one backward.

POP QUIZ:

"Without the Judgment of Charity, what do our communication filters tend to be looking for? How does this impact the rebuilding of trust?"

MUST WE TRI? MORE THAN ONCE?

TRI is an acronym for "Take Responsibility & Initiative." A peacemaker must not passively let others take responsibility for pursuing peace. They must be willing to be among "the first steppers."

Matthew 18 teaches us that we must try more than once. Jesus also teaches us there that we must be willing to take responsibility and initiative to ask for the help of others as we escalate the care-fronting. To not do so, is to sin by omission.

Conflict can be caused by other's sins, our sins, or a combination of the two. In all cases we are mandated to pursue peace. We must be willing to "Take Responsibility & Initiative." Responsibility for our methods AND our motives, including our efforts to give the Judgment of Charity. And, initiative in seeking to make a way to restore the damaged or broken relationship.

This mandate is not fulfilled by giving it one try, or even two. If we have not humbled ourselves and asked for help to escalate the care-fronting, we still bear the burden of NOT fulfilling the Bible's teaching to be a peacemaker.

We often excuse our giving up by saying things like, *"It wouldn't make any difference anyway. They won't listen, and they certainly won't change."* Unfortunately, this is a statement of judgment made by one being judgmental. Doing the right thing is not contingent upon whether we think it will work. We are responsible for our obedience, NOT their choices in response.

POP QUIZ:

"Are we released from the responsibility to take initiative in pursuing peace, even when we are not 'the leader' or 'the person with power?'"

WHEN TO JUDGE

Often in conflict, people will ask you to judge whether they are right or not, implicitly suggesting you take their side. It is usually wisest to not be a judge but a peacemaker.

The time to take the role of a judge is when both sides have agreed to have you act in binding arbitration. 1 Corinthians 6:1-8 would be an example of this.

People are often pulled into conflict by others who want them to act like a judge, a detective, or a hit-man. We hear the evidence, only presented by the one side who is talking with us, and then are asked for a judgment. *"Don't you agree that this is the meanest thing they could do?"*

Other times we may be asked to be a detective, to go snoop around for more facts. This is like the old middle school, *"Go see if Sally likes me."* People in authority, like elders and pastors, are often put in the position of hearing about a conflict between others and then being asked, *"So, what are YOU going to do about it?"* The monkey of responsibility suddenly tries to jump to their back, putting them in a position of judge and jury.

When either party in a conflict feels like we, as a mediator, have been the other person's advocate, we will have little ability to help solve the problem. An exception to this would be when conflict has been escalated through the Matthew 18 steps and there is no resolution. Using 1 Corinthians 6 as a model, the parties can then ask for binding arbitration. In essence, they are asking other believers to act a judge over their conflict.

POP QUIZ:

"What is the difference between someone filling the role of mediator vs. the role of judge?"

MOTIVES & METHODS

Methods are outward actions, done or left undone, that we can witness with our eyes and ears.

Motives are inward intentions, that only God understands perfectly. An individual tends to give themselves the Judgment of Charity about their own motives.

An easy way to remember this is to think of M&M candies. The candy shell is the METHODS we can see. The chocolate inside is the MOTIVE we cannot see.

Critical to understanding how to "fight with the Judgment of Charity" are the concepts of Motives and Methods. We must ask for God's help to give someone the Judgment of Charity regarding their motives (their heart), while holding them accountable for their methods (their actions).

When we lose the Judgment of Charity, we start to assume that the other person's motives are bad, or at least, not good. This assumption is often the result of "mind-reading," thinking we can know what another person's intentions are without them telling us.

We also "pigeon-hole" people by assuming that certain methods must also mean certain motives. These linkages are usually made based on past experiences we have had.

Motives and Methods also relate to speaking the truth in love. We must communicate truth about another's methods, while being gentle and gracious, communicating love by assuming the best possible motives on their part.

An example would be when I bought 60 tulips for my wife's 60th birthday. The guy standing in front of me at the checkout says, "Wow! What did you do wrong?!" The two ladies helping me check-out looked for my response. When I told them why I was buying the six bunches, they both gave a verbal sigh of delight.

My method was buying 60 tulips at one time. No one "knew" my motive. The gentleman in front of me assumed that my motive was to get out of trouble (though, perhaps he was just kidding around). The ladies did not express a judgment of my motives based on their assumptions. Rather, they waited until I made clear my motives of honoring my wife on her birthday. They then used the method of "sighing" to express delight (or so I assumed).

We tend to give ourselves grace, excusing our poor or confusing methods, because we have good motives or intentions. This is also often tied to our self-talk. We might say in our heads, *"If you only knew how hard I tried* (motives), *you wouldn't be giving me such a hard time about what the visible outcomes were* (methods)."

POP QUIZ:

"Are someone's tone of voice and facial expression a method or a motive?"

SPEAK THE TRUTH IN LOVE

"Truthing in love" is what the unified but diverse church will be doing when she is living out the calling of Jesus. Ephesians 4:15 is often translated, "Speaking the truth in love." How can we practically do this?

One helpful tool is to speak **love** by expressing the Judgment of Charity that we have towards another's **motives.** This is then followed up by a clear "**truth** statement" about what we see as to their **methods.**

Even if we know we should speak the truth in love, we often need help in knowing HOW to do so. When we only speak "in love," we often are wishy-washy and unclear. We tend to take the blame for the way things are and do not communicate assertively enough to really pursue peace. Speaking "in truth" tends to come across as harsh, demanding and even judgmental. We act like the conflict is not about a relationship but about a business transaction.

When we LOVINGLY express the Judgment of Charity the Holy Spirit has helped us to gain about the other party's MOTIVES, we help lower defenses and make a way. This is then followed up by TRUTHFULLY telling the other party how their METHODS have impacted us. We try to do this without pigeon-holing their methods with what the judgment of bitterness and blame might guess about their motives.

Some have suggested that we make a "love sandwich" by adding another layer of love, confirming to them that we have the Judgment of Charity. This would especially helpful for those who tend to be more task oriented and assertive. Or for those who have been injustice gathering for some time and would therefore tend to be harsher, even without trying to do so.

POP QUIZ:

"We are to speak love about which one, people's motives or methods?"

COMMUNICATION FILTERS

Composed of our **pasts,** our **self-talk** and influenced by our **sinful selves,** our filters impact how we interpret what others say and do. And they impact how we try to communicate to others about our judgments regarding what they have done or left undone.

ALL of our communication, both sent and received, is filtered. Filters are the grid through which a person passes their experiences and their attempts to communicate their reactions to those experiences. What makes things so interesting is that all of us have different filters. Even those who grew up in the same family have differences that are influenced by their birth order, as well as their gender, physical appearance, mental capacities, and much more. Anyone who has been to another culture and has tried to communicate will attest to the reality of filters.

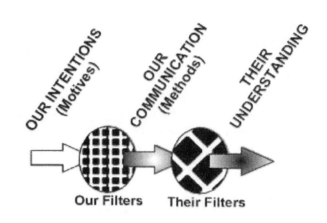

OUR INTENTIONS (Motives)   OUR COMMUNICATION (Methods)   THEIR UNDERSTANDING

Our Filters   Their Filters

When we give others the Judgment of Charity, we make the active choice to believe that their methods make sense to them, as they see them through their filters.

When effort is taken to understand others' filters and to explore why we have the ones we do, great progress can be made in the pursuit of peace. These conversations tend to be more learning than about blaming. Understanding a bit more about another's filters does not mean we excuse their methods when we feel they are inappropriate, Rather, we can approach them with greater gentleness. We often can also communicate better when we know what filters our efforts to communicate are going through.

The concept of filters should also make us more humble in conflict. Because we tend to give ourselves the Judgment of Charity about our motives, we often do not carefully examine our own filters, assuming that we have a perfect grasp on the facts. After all, we imagine that our filters do not impact our ability to judge because we are "objective."

> **POP QUIZ:**
>
> "How is the presence or absence of the Judgment of Charity part of our filtering of other people?"

MIND-READING & PIGEON-HOLING

MIND-READING assumes either we or others should be able to know what another person is thinking without them directly telling us.

PIGEON-HOLING assumes that certain methods a person uses always puts them into a certain cubby-hole. "This means that!"

Communication breaks down in many ways. Two of the most overarching problems are MIND-READING and PIGEON-HOLING.

We MIND-READ when we imagine that we can read another person's mind, especially their motives, without them telling us. The flip-side of this is also a problem: we think the other person should be able to read OUR minds without us saying anything to them.

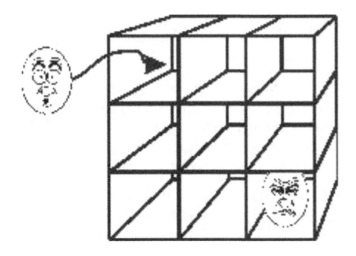

PIGEON-HOLING is almost impossible for us not to do. We all tend to fit our perception of other people's methods into our assumptions of what they mean, especially about another person's motives. For example, when a person is quiet it may be easy for some to put them into the box labeled "upset."

We need to <u>become aware of our assumptions</u> of "this means that." And then we need to <u>check it out</u>, asking the other person what they mean by the method we just witnessed.

POP QUIZ:

"When we assume we can read another person's mind, what do we tend to stop doing?"

STOP, LOOK, AND LISTEN

Using a railroad crossing as a memory tool, three important biblical steps to stirring up the Judgment of Charity are highlighted.

When we reach a conflict crossroads in a relationship, we should take the time to prayerfully STOP, LOOK, AND LISTEN.

We must ask the Holy Spirit to help us STOP judging the motives of the other person.

We need to LOOK to their interests and perspectives, seeking to understand them. This will require that we LISTEN to them first, before making it our objective to share with them our righteous indignation.

*Therefore let us **stop** passing judgment on one another. Instead, make up your mind not to put any stumbling block or obstacle in your brother's way.*

*Each of you should **look** not only to your own interests, but also to the interests of others.*

*My dear brothers, take note of this: Everyone should be quick to **listen**, slow to speak and slow to become angry, for man's anger does not bring about the righteous life that God desires.*

Romans 14:13, Philippians 2:4, James 1:19-20 NIV

POP QUIZ:

"How is looking to the interests of others an expression of the Judgment of Charity?"

GOSSIP

There are three warning lights that help us know when we are slipping into gossip.

1) We are talking **behind someone's back**.

2) We are saying **bad things** about someone.

3) We are sharing but **not for the good purpose**. We are not really seeking help for directly going to the person about whom we are saying bad things.

The common evil of gossip ruins many relationships. Instead of dealing directly with the person with whom we have a conflict, we talk to a third party. We may imply that it is now their responsibility to deal with the conflict on our behalf. Or, we could be just using them as a place to vent our frustrations. Either way, the speaking of bad things behind someone's back without the purpose of pursuing peace is sinful.

Matthew Mitchell wrote Resisting Gossip in 2013. This book is a great resource to help us conquer the problem of a wagging tongue. My definition of gossip builds on Mitchell's, but changes the third warning light, as I call it. He said that the third component of gossip was that it was "from a bad heart." As we have seen in Scripture and in experience, most of us give ourselves the Judgment of Charity most of the time. Thus, it would be very rare that we would judge ourselves to be guilty of gossip. After all, we *"meant well"* and *"only shared so that they could pray with me about the situation."*

The method of gossip, even when we imagine it was from a good heart, puts the third party in the awkward position of needing to care-front us. Since "gossipers should be hung, one from the ear and one from the tongue," they do not want to be guilty of gossip by listening to it. They hopefully will be gentle in pointing out what we are doing. They will have to cut off the conversation unless we are willing to have them equip us to go directly to the person we have a problem with.

Gossip, when uncovered by the person being talked about, raises their defenses. It is very challenging to give the Judgment of Charity to someone when they have been complaining about us to others. The process of gossip also tends to solidify us in our judgment of the other person's motives. This happens because we have verbalized our assumptions or because the third party jumps in and gives us their (usually negative) assumptions of the erring person's motives.

We must be willing to escalate with the help of others but gossiping and venting our feelings is not the help we need.

POP QUIZ:

"What is the difference between gossiping by 'venting' and seeking help from another to escalate care-fronting?"

HEARSAY

Hearsay is what we've heard said but have not ourselves witnessed. This is **not admissible in a court of law,** nor should it be in our daily lives.

Hearsay easily falls into the category of gossip. We may be **tempted to treat it like evidence** because we know and trust the person telling us. But, we have not witnessed the actions. We have only "heard said" that they happened.

Many conflict situations are confused through "hearsay." This is especially true of when we are being pulled into others' battles. Often tied to gossip, we are tempted to treat what we heard someone say as the gospel truth, even though we were not witnesses of the situation. We have only "heard them say" that such-and-such happened.

We want to believe that the person telling us is trustworthy and not a gossip. We are still giving THEM the Judgment of Charity and so we want to believe what they tell us. However, unless they are talking with us about how to go address the situation, they are guilty of gossip.

If we go care-front someone based on what we have heard someone else say about them, we have treated hearsay like "evidence" of their guilt. What we can do when we are told hearsay is to raise our antennae and be wary to see if we are witnesses of any evidence on which we can follow-up.

POP QUIZ:

"Why does confronting people based on hearsay tend to greatly raise their defenses?"

When Jesus went about telling of the kingdom of God, He told people to repent and believe. The common misunderstanding about the difference between repentance and the fruits of repentance leads to a great roadblock to pursuing peace.

There are Christ-followers who think that repentance is a work, and since we are not saved by works, we do not need to repent. That same thinking then applies to whom we forgive. We are told to forgive them whether they repent or not. However, when we realize that repentance is a change of HEART, not a cleaning up of ourselves before we come to Jesus for salvation, things greatly change.

Why does God require repentance AND belief (faith) to receive forgiveness through Christ? Because He is the only one Who can see a person's heart. Only He can immediately know if a person has turned away from their sin AND turned to Christ in faith (two sides of the same coin).

If we do not differentiate repentance from its fruits, then we have set up our justification before God to be earned in some part by our works. The fruits of repentance are <u>not</u> part of the grounds of forgiveness and salvation. If we grasp these concepts correctly, we understand that the visible fruits of repentance are merely what will show up in time because the heart has truly repented and believed. If there are no fruits then there was no repentance.

In our forgiveness of another person, we choose to forgive them based on their voiced expression of repentance. That is, they have told us that they have had a change of heart. Since we cannot see their hearts, our decision to forgive is done in obedience to Jesus' teaching, entrusting the ultimate judgment to Him. Since we cannot see the heart's repentance, it is understandable that our observing the fruits of repentance would be necessary for us to know that the other party has indeed repented. This is the process of forgiveness where trust is rebuilt.

POP QUIZ:

"What is the difference between how God knows, and how people know, if someone has truly repented?"

CYCLE OF CONFLICT

On-going conflict tends to follow a basic pattern of five stages. These stages are:

- SOMETHING'S WRONG? Also called "tension development." Parties are uncertain what is the issue, but they have a feeling something is amiss.

- WHAT'S WRONG? At this stage the issue is much more clearly defined. We can mark it with an "X." Some refer to this as "role dilemma" because there is uncertainty about who should do what about the problem at hand.

- YOU'RE WRONG! Conflict deteriorates from being issue-focused toward seeing the other person as the root of the problem. Also called "injustice gathering" because folks start to make lists of additional evidence, that in their minds "prove" the other person is at fault. Over time the initial issue is often lost.

- LET'S FIGHT! In on-going conflict that has been stuck in gathering injustices and hurts, this "confrontation" can be set off with a relatively small "presenting issue."

- WHO WON? The final stage that evidences some sort of "resolution." This can range from an outcome that is healthy to division and abandonment of the relationship.

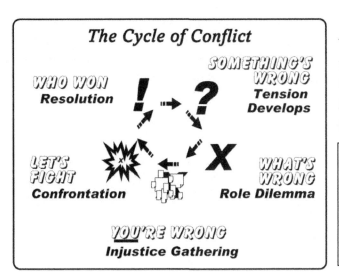

The Cycle of Conflict

WHO WON
Resolution

SOMETHING'S WRONG
Tension Develops

LET'S FIGHT
Confrontation

WHAT'S WRONG
Role Dilemma

YOU'RE WRONG
Injustice Gathering

The Cycle of Conflict is a tool that provides a way to communicate empathy and hope. It can be helpfully shared after listening to folks give their answers to, "What do you think the problem is in your relationship?"

POP QUIZ:

Unless the conflict has reached the LET'S FIGHT! Stage, do all the participants necessarily agree what stage they are in?

INCREASING TENSION'S IMPACTS
through the stages of conflict

As a person moves through the cycle of conflict, usually there is an increase in felt tension. This increase tends to influence us to make "big conclusions from little facts." Three impacts include:

- Our communication filters tend to "close down" and our defensive shields tend to go up.

- Our focus changes from looking at the other person's Methods, to judging another person's Motives.

- Often unwittingly, we will change our style of dealing with conflict. Our preferred style did not seem to be working so we adapt.

The Cycle of Conflict should be a reminder to "not let the sun go down on our anger." Dealing with conflicts sooner is healthier. To not deal with them is to allow conflict to move past the safe zone of the first two stages.

We often will not discuss conflict in stage one because we do not want to make a mountain out of a molehill. When there is greater clarity in stage two, many of us find ourselves afraid of hurting others or being hurt.

The first two stages provide the greatest opportunity for an easier positive outcome. Our filters may have constricted a bit and we might be tempted to read into another's actions. But, we usually have not lost the Judgment of Charity towards the other party's motives. We have not begun to gather evidence that goes beyond the problem of the issue at hand to the person themselves.

The increasing tension also has an impact on our choice of which style of conflict we will use. Often it is not a conscious choice, just a reaction to the tension. Our transition to our secondary, and perhaps tertiary style, encourages us to be aware of what we tend to do under pressure. This knowledge will help to intentionally choose the best style for pursuing peace.

POP QUIZ:

Why is it so dangerous to allow conflict to move out of the first two stages, to the point where the Judgment of Charity is eroded in stage three?

GRAPHIC: IMPACTS OF THE CYCLE

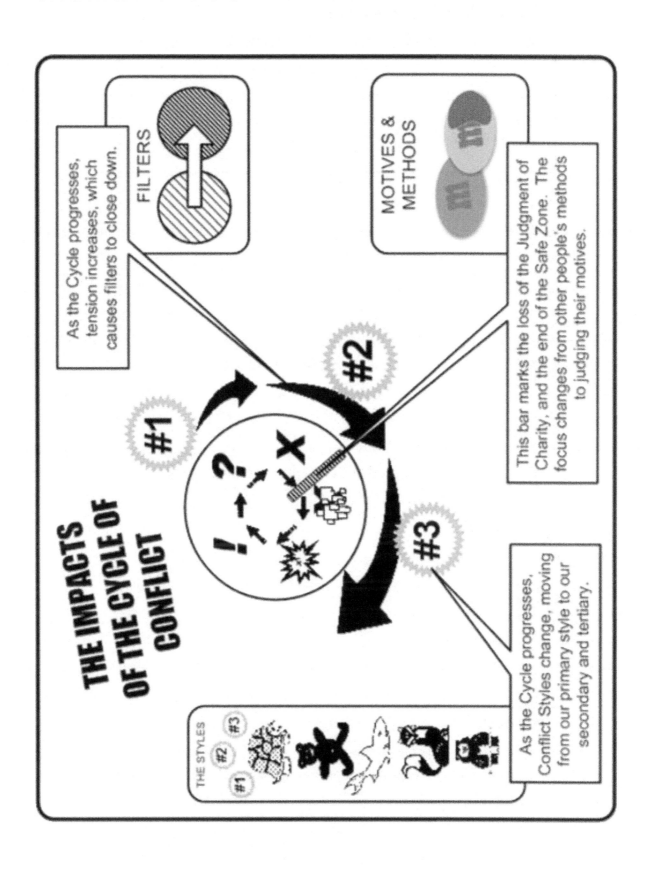

THE IMPACTS OF THE CYCLE OF CONFLICT

FILTERS

As the Cycle progresses, tension increases, which causes filters to close down.

MOTIVES & METHODS

This bar marks the loss of the Judgment of Charity, and the end of the Safe Zone. The focus changes from other people's methods to judging their motives.

THE STYLES

As the Cycle progresses, Conflict Styles change, moving from our primary style to our secondary and tertiary.

SOMETHING'S WRONG
Stage One in the Cycle of Conflict

Also called "tension development." One or both parties feels a loss of freedom in the relationship, but they often don't know why. It would be best if the individual who feels the loss would "check it out" by sharing their concern and asking for clarification.

Something's Wrong? Note that the label is in the form of a question. At this early stage of conflict there often is an uncertainty, a wondering if something is amiss. Some call this stage "tension development" because initial feelings of tension arise. Stress comes from a perceived loss of freedom in the relationship. Our radar has picked up a signal that we are unsure of.

"Did that door slam because they are mad or because the wind caught it? Are they not making eye contact with me because I said something stupid or am I being overly-sensitive? That tone of voice does not seem to fit what they are saying . . . which do they really mean?" Questions like this flit through our minds.

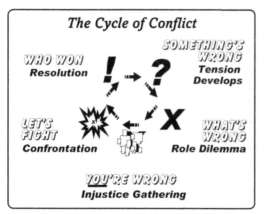

The Cycle of Conflict

Many people do nothing at this stage of conflict because they "don't want to make a mountain out of a mole-hill." Not "checking it out" with the other person denies that we are already having a discussion WITHIN our own minds about the situation. This self-talk does not have the benefit of the other person's input.

POP QUIZ:

"Why should we CHECK IT OUT with the other person when we first feel a loss of freedom in our relationship with them?"

WHAT'S WRONG
Stage Two in the Cycle of Conflict

Also called "role dilemma." At this stage the core issue in the conflict could be marked with an "X." The problem is that there often is a dilemma about whose role it is to bring the issue up.

This is the last safe stage of conflict because the focus is still on the issue (the "What" that is wrong) rather than on the other person.

WHAT'S WRONG? At this second stage, the conflict has a bit more clarity. The issue at hand is right in front of us. That is why in the graphic of the cycle we mark it with an "X." We now know what was or was not done. Perhaps it came out into the open through a direct confrontation. Often it is exposed to the light through some witty sarcasm or indirect reference. In any case, there is a "role dilemma" because it seems uncertain who should do what. *"Should I bring it up? Should I just "bear up" with it?"*

At this point, many do not want to care-front the conflict because they dread it. Our past experiences with conflict have often been negative. Perhaps if we just *"ignore it, it will go away."*

Because the uncertainty of stage one has now morphed into an "actual" conflict, it is critical "not to let the sun go down on our anger." By dealing promptly with the issue, we lessen the chances for the Judgment of Charity to be lost.

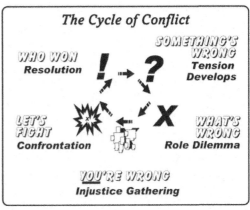

Biblically, we are told to go to a brother who we believe is sinning against us (see Matthew 18:15-17). We are also told to leave our worship offering on the altar while we go deal with a brother who has something against us (see Matthew 5:23-26). So, whether we think we are being wronged or have done wrong, Jesus expects us to initiate pursuing peace. In a sense, this removes the role dilemma, making the Christian's role one of "peacemaker" in all circumstances.

POP QUIZ:

Why is the "What's Wrong?" stage of conflict the last "safe" stage?

YOU'RE WRONG
Stage Three in the Cycle of Conflict

This stage has been referred to as "injustice gathering." The difference from stage two, "What's Wrong?", is the focus of the conflict. Instead of keying into the "What," now the attention moves to the "Who." Specifically, the "You."

Evidence is gathered in this often "quiet" stage. Like a prosecuting attorney collecting evidence for their case, we look for "proof" that the problem is not just the "What," but rather the character and motives of the other person.

YOU'RE WRONG! This stage marks the deterioration of conflict. We have let the sun go down on our anger and hurt. Because we have not dealt with the tension of stage one, nor the specific issue of stage two, we now enter a quiet stage that can last for years.

The third stage is marked by "injustice gathering." I call it the "list making stage." The lists tend to cover up the "X" of the issue. In this stage, individuals or groups are collecting evidence to prove their point. But, the point is not necessarily the issue uncovered in the second stage.

The evidence being gathered is used to make a case against the Motives of the person or parties who offended them. This evidence may not hold up in court. It is often hearsay (what was "heard said" as the fruit of gossip) or circumstantial. The sources of information and their reliability become less and less consequential as this stage lingers on. We just want "proof and more proof" about how wrong the other person is (in their Motives, not just their Methods).

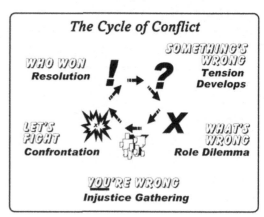

The Cycle of Conflict

WHO WON
Resolution

SOMETHING'S WRONG
Tension Develops

LET'S FIGHT
Confrontation

WHAT'S WRONG
Role Dilemma

YOU'RE WRONG
Injustice Gathering

Up to this point you may be assuming that both parties have walked through the first three stages together. One person may still be at the first stage while the other one is in the second year of being at this blaming, "You're wrong!" stage.

POP QUIZ:

How does the "You're Wrong" stage "add up a record of wrongs," in violation of 1 Corinthian's 13's definition of love?

LET'S FIGHT!
Stage Four in the Cycle of Conflict

This stage has been referred to as "confrontation." However, conflict can be helpfully "care-fronted" long before this stage.

Often the "fight" is triggered by some precipitating event. This little issue ignites the stored-up injustices and there is an explosion. Very little effort is usually made dealing with the current or originating issues. Most of the energy tends to be directed toward blaming the other party. This venting of frustration rarely stays focused on their methods, but often hurtfully thrusts accusations against their motives.

LET'S FIGHT! The fourth stage brings everyone up to the same point (even if they were not there before). This is the open conflict stage. Sometimes referred to as the "confrontation" stage. I believe this is a misnomer since the conflict can and should be confronted long before.

When this point is reached, it is often initiated by a small precipitating event. In the graphic you see an explosion and within it a small "X." This is the small spark that sets off the forest fire that consumes all the fuel that has been stored up in the injustice gathering of the YOU'RE WRONG! stage.

After teaching some of this material in a day-long workshop for the Human Resource Department of a university, I was approached by one of the participants. She had taken the 8-hour seminar under the pretense that it was for work. She said the real reason was because her boyfriend had just moved out. To my knowledge she was not a follower of Christ, so my main interest did not focus on the immorality of cohabitation.

I asked her, "What do you think caused him to leave?" Her answer will forever be burned into my mind. "Because I left a spoon in the sink." This was only the proverbial "straw that broke the camel's back." Her boyfriend had been gathering injustices for a long time. The spoon in the sink pushed the conflict into the "LET'S FIGHT!" stage.

I use the term "fight" because it carries a negative sense to it. Not all conflict is "fighting" (though it is hard to convince some folks of that). Conflict can and does get ugly. It is this ugliness that most of us dread. That dread keeps us from living out the Judgment of Charity. It is critical that we learn how to "care-front" conflict long before this hideousness shows itself.

> **POP QUIZ:**
>
> If conflict is not care-fronted before it reaches the "Let's Fight" stage, where does the focus of attention lie, on the other party's methods or motives?

WHO WON?
Stage Five in the Cycle of Conflict

This stage can be called "resolution." After the conflict moves to the open, there is some sort of resolution. It could be positive or negative. Without the restoration of the Judgment of Charity, the conflict often has a winner and a loser. The relationship may continue but the bonds of love usually have been weakened.

At this point, the cycle of conflict is an over-simplification. Many conflicts spiral back to further injustice gathering, often with less Judgment of Charity than before. Or, there is a "wait and see" attitude that continues to look for the other party to mess up and prove that our assessment of their motives and hearts was correct.

WHO WON? The terminology for the last stage reflects a win-lose mentality in the conflict. After fights there are always winners and losers. But there usually is some sort of "resolution" as well, which is a title sometimes given to this point in the cycle.

The resolution often is divorce or domination. Sometimes it is a renegotiation with a continuing sense of a standoff, like what happens in a messy management-union situation in the work world. As these adjustments to the relationship are made, they often yield a more defensive posture on the part of the individuals. This means that the next cycle of conflict is poised to get poisonous even quicker than the previous go-around.

Often the "Let's Fight" stage yielded only a "venting" of hurt feelings and defensiveness. If so, then the conflict can enter into the "Death Spiral," moving back to the "You're Wrong" stage to gather further ammo against the character of the other person. All this evidence is used to blame them for the conflict, even for our choices. "You made me act like that," is a refrain that will often increase in frequency as the "Death Spiral" is spun through again and again.

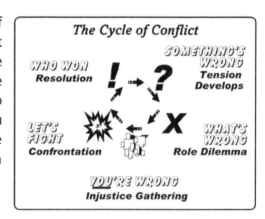

POP QUIZ:

Must the "resolution" of the "Who Won?" stage of conflict be positive? Why?

GRAPHIC: CYCLE OF CONFLICT WITH LABELS

Something is wrong

Tension Develops and we begin to lose "freedom" in the relationship. We start to think that something is not quite right, but we may not be able to put our finger on it. We often don't bring it up because we don't want to "make a mountain out of a molehill."

What is wrong?

The focus remains on the methods used that produced the conflict. This is also called the **Role Dilemma** stage. There is often confusion about who should bring the conflict up for discussion. We often don't bring it up because it is better to "let sleeping dogs lie."

The Judgment of Charity line. Safer conflict happens before this line. After crossing this line, we start assuming bad things about the other person's motives.

You are wrong!

The **Injustice Gathering** stage when we look for further proof that the problem is not just the other person's methods but their motives. Because our filters are more and more clogged by the loss of the Judgment of Charity, we easily read negative motives into the other party's methods. This quiet stage can go on for a long time.

The Death Spiral.

Often conflict will explode into a "fight" (the Let's Fight stage), but there will be no clear resolution. Anger and frustration are "vented" but no action steps of change happen. This moves us back into the "You are wrong!" stage for further injustice gathering.

Who won?

Sometimes called the **Resolution** stage. This does not mean all conflicts are "resolved" well. Rather, the relationship is usually changed in some way, either finding peace or some level of separation from each other.

Let's fight!

Also call the **Confrontation** stage. While often labeled "confrontation," conflict can and should be confronted *before* losing the Judgment of Charity. This loud stage is often precipitated by a little "X" of an offending method. Focusing just on that presenting issue misses dealing with the bitterness that has been developing during the injustice gathering, "You are wrong!" stage.

INJUSTICE GATHERING

Another name for the "You're Wrong" stage in the cycle of conflict.

Also, an apt description of what happens when the Judgment of Charity is lost or weakened. We tend to quietly gather evidence that our hypothesis is true, the problem really is the other person.

These perceived injustices are filtered through self-talk, which has already turned negative by this stage of the cycle.

When the Judgment of Charity starts to fade, conflict usually moves from "What's Wrong?" to the "You're Wrong!" stage. The problem is no longer a person's methods, as much as it is the assumption that they have bad motives. It is at this point that we are tempted to "injustice gather," accumulating evidence that the problem is the other person. We judge them to be mean, thoughtless, self-consumed, or whatever.

Injustice gathering is also another name for the "You're Wrong!" stage in the cycle of conflict. We may think we are only gathering "facts" to support our case. But, we tend to forget that we see these facts through our filters. If we have lost the Judgment of Charity, our filters are now set to capture all the negatives and by-pass or misread any potential positives.

When we release our bullet-points of evidence found during our gathering of injustices, the out loud blaming starts. There are severe costs when this begins. The attack, adversarial posture usually puts others on the defensive. We tend to stop listening and looking to the interests of others. We do not seek further understanding, but rather want to make others understand us. Things tend to seem black and white, especially if the injustice gathering has been going on for some time.

POP QUIZ:

"Why do we 'injustice gather' when we have lost the Judgment of Charity?"

THE DEATH SPIRAL
and the Cycle of Conflict

The Death Spiral occurs when conflict goes back and forth between stages three and four, "You're Wrong" and "Let's Fight." Things get very public and out in the open but then move back into a time of quiet when further injustices are gathered.

When the Judgment of Charity has not been restored, even changes in methods that the parties have committed to will be looked at through a filter of anticipated failure. That is, we will be looking for the other person to mess up and "prove" to us that they never really did mean what they said about changing.

Like the vortex in our bathtubs when we let out the water, we can easily be sucked down into a death spiral of conflict. While there may be many moments of confronting the conflict, when there is never a healthy resolution, the infection lingers on.

Instead of each party owning the part of the conflict that is theirs and extending forgiveness for the other party's trespasses, there is only a "fight." We make our case or defend ourselves. We cast blame on the other person, even for the things we've done or left undone.

This "venting" may make us feel a bit better for a little while. When the other folks continue to do, or not do, what they now should clearly understand bothers us, the death spiral picks up speed. *"How could they not change?! Now they know how much it bugs me when they do that. I just told them so in no uncertain terms."*

Deeper into the spiral it gets harder and harder not to judge the other party's motives as anything but malicious and unloving. The renewed injustice gathering further erodes any remnants of the Judgment of Charity. This makes any further confrontations less about learning and understanding the other person's perspective. It becomes all about stating our case a bit louder and stronger.

When we are caught in the death spiral, we need to seek help quickly. We probably have already violated the biblical principle of not letting the sun go down on our anger. If we allow the conflict to spin out of control, it may be almost impossible to pull out of it. Even the styles of conflict resolution we end up using will be unconscious choices, as we grasp for anything that might work.

THE DEATH SPIRAL

Judgment of Charity deteriorates

POP QUIZ:

After conflict has been confronted ("Let's Fight!") it may not really be resolved and cycle back to injustice gathering ("You're Wrong!")? Why is this so dangerous?

THE DEATH SPIRAL
A Self-Assessment

It is easy for some to be sucked into the Death Spiral, even blaming ourselves for all the conflict. We need the Holy Spirit to give us an "Aha-Moment" to show us if we are in this dangerous vortex. If so, we need to be humble enough to get help right away.

AM I IN THE "DEATH SPIRAL" OF CONFLICT?

INSTRUCTIONS: For each of the actions described below, circle the number in the column that reflects the approximate frequency that you practice this behavior. Total your scores to reflect to what degree you are in danger.

It can be helpful to focus on a single key relationship (such as a spouse or friend) as you think through these behaviors. *We may be in the "death spiral" with one person or several, but rarely will it be true for "everyone" in our lives.*

DESCRIPTION OF BEHAVIOR	APPROXIMATE FREQUENCY				
	Almost always	Much of the time	Some of the time	On occasion	Very Rarely
I go to bed with a measurable anger or hurt over unresolved conflict.	5	4	3	2	1
I say, "It's OK," when I know it really is not. It's my burden to bear.	5	4	3	2	1
I consider that a conflict is over when I have verbally won the argument and the other party gives in.	5	4	3	2	1
I find myself thinking about, even dwelling on, people's bad motives that I believe lie behind what they did.	5	4	3	2	1
I make a mental list of all the things the other person has done that proves to me that they really are to blame.	5	4	3	2	1
When we try to talk about conflicts, I respond to their explanations and rationale with a, "Yeah, BUT . . ." (at least in my mind).	5	4	3	2	1
When we have a "new" conflict, I work hard to think of all the possible "reasonable" motives that <u>could</u> lie behind others' irritating methods.	1	2	3	4	5
When a conflict is deep and hurtful, I spend extended time praying for the other person (and not just prayers of cursing).	1	2	3	4	5
I know that it is my duty as a Christian to extend forgiveness, and I say I do that. Yet, the speed at which I pull up the list of the other's past wrongs makes it clear I certainly have not "forgotten."	5	4	3	2	1
I say that the issue is dealt with and that I have no bitterness or anger, BUT I am adamant about keeping my distance (physically or emotionally) from the other person.	5	4	3	2	1
I walk on egg-shells after we've had a conflict. We don't talk about it and pretend it is gone, but I'm scared that I will set them off again.	5	4	3	2	1
I catch myself telling others bad things about the person I've had conflict with. I may say it is to help me deal with the conflict, but I never really take any action steps after these "venting sessions."	5	4	3	2	1
TOTAL SCORE (add all the circled scores together)					

This is not a scientific test but a tool to cause personal reflection. The "grading scale" is only a teaching tool, not an absolute predictor of the future.
12-20 = Fantastic, you are NOT letting the sun go down on conflict; 21-30 = Good job but be careful, remember that unresolved conflict is cumulative; 31-40 = There are some strong negative patterns developing, consider getting help; 41-50 = You are likely being pulled down into the spiral and may feel there is nothing you can do. Get help soon; 51-60 = You are further down the hole than you can imagine. If you don't act soon, the relationship could be doomed.

TWO TENSIONS OF CONFLICT

LOVE/RELATIONSHIPS. One needs to have some sort of relationship with another person or group to be in conflict with them. The relative value one places on these relationships makes up the first tension of conflict.

TRUTH/GOALS. The second tension needed for a conflict to exist is for the parties to have some goals they want to see happen, or some truth that they believe needs to be upheld.

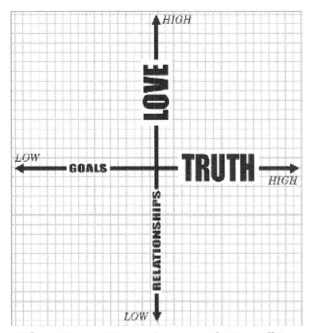

The Two Tensions of Conflict

At a basic level, all conflict is an interplay between tensions. Relationships and Goals, both have to matter for conflict to surface. If we do not care about a relationship, we can simply abandon it when we do not get enough of our way. If we don't have any goals of how things should be done, then we can just give in to those we want a relationship with. Neither of these extremes are healthy in the long-term.

More biblical terminology for these two tensions would be Truth and Love. In Ephesians 4:15, we are told how the diverse but unified Church should operate. They need to be "truthing in love." Learning to speak the truth about our goals, in a loving manner than strengthens our relationships, is the challenge of a peacemaker.

These two axes of tension are reflected most beautifully in Jesus Christ. John 1:17 tells us that He came full of grace AND truth. God so loved the world that He gave us His Son. But, the truth of the gospel message is that those who will not humble themselves and trust the Son will face the holy wrath of God against their sin.

POP QUIZ:

About which tension should we be gently assertive?
About which one should we be graciously responsive?

FIVE STYLES OF CONFLICT RESOLUTION

Integrated with the Two Tensions

LOW LOVE – LOW TRUTH. The "Turtle" <u>avoids</u> conflict. They do so by withdrawing from the relationship to some degree. Over time, others will take their non-opposition/non-involvement for granted.

HIGH LOVE – LOW TRUTH. The "Teddy Bear" <u>accommodates</u> others in conflict. They will give in to others' goals in order to keep the relationship. This may initially be done out of love, but it is a difficult posture to maintain over the long-term.

LOW LOVE – HIGH TRUTH. The "Shark" sees conflict as a <u>competition</u>. Someone has to win, and someone has to lose. Though they may think of themselves as benevolent dictators, Sharks tend to be lacking in gentleness and responsiveness to the needs of others.

HALF HIGH LOVE – HALF HIGH TRUTH. The "Fox" is one who <u>negotiates</u> their way through conflict. Their "win-a-little/lose-a-little" style works when selling homes and buying used cars. Yet, because there are rarely open about their true motives and intentions, it is difficult to build a relationship of strong trust with them.

HIGH LOVE – HIGH TRUTH. The wise "Owl" seeks to <u>collaborate</u> whenever possible by listening carefully to others, seeking to understand their perspectives, while remaining firm about his own goals. He seeks to gently speak the truth in love.

The Two Tensions of Conflict

The Five Styles all have their place. There are times when we should choose each one. But, in a long-term relationship, the only style that will produce the maximum health is that of an Owl. Only the Owl style will encourage the other party to act like an Owl.

Very rarely will people consistently be at the extremes described. Our styles can and do change, depending on the relationship and the tension level.

POP QUIZ:

Why is the Owl style the best long-term way to handle conflict?

TURTLES

AVOIDING conflict is how turtles deal with problems. There are some problems that are not worth dealing with.

As I was with my children (when they were younger) near the river that runs by our home, we found a turtle. It was a very pretty, little turtle. My kids were thrilled when I picked it up by its shell. We did not intend to hurt the turtle; we just wanted to say hello and see how he was doing. His response was typical of every turtle that I have ever held or looked at or gently poked at with a stick (snapping turtles are dangerous!). Turtles stick their head in their shell, along with their feet and tail. All that is left is shell and a wary eye peering out sideways.

Such is the response of many people to conflict. For most of us, conflict of any seriousness engages the production of the "fight or flight" hormone of adrenaline. Turtles choose (sometimes unconsciously) to respond to the adrenaline in their system by "flight." They run from conflict; they avoid it at all costs. Sometimes these individuals physically get sick and must leave the conflict setting. Other times they become recluses, pulling into their own shells, seeking to protect themselves the only way that they know.

If you were to list some of the descriptions that fit the typical turtle, they would include: passive, abdicating, they leave conflict and lose their goals, they tend to be non-cooperative in defining the conflict or in seeking and implementing the solutions arrived at. On our two-tension graph, the TURTLE would be put at the extreme of LOW-LOW. They do not place a very high priority on either the relationships or the goals. Their main aim is self-preservation by AVOIDING conflict wherever possible.

We should not be too hard on Turtles. Many times, their style of managing conflict has been learned through their childhood experiences. Perhaps as a child it was the only style that was available to them that would allow them to survive. Parents that are too harsh, abusive relationships, cruel circumstances may force a child into their shell. That way they could at least make it through to another day.

POP QUIZ:

What is the key word that describes a Turtle's way of dealing with conflict?

TEDDY BEARS

__ACCOMMODATING__ others' goals is how Teddy Bears deal with problems. Often acting out of love, but sometimes out of fear, these individuals are willing to make the sacrifices needed to maintain the relationship they want (or feel they need).

Teddy Bears tend to be my favorite people, at least in the short run. Like their mascot, they are warm and fuzzy folks who love to be hugged. They tend to have a smile on their faces. And they certainly do not want to be left out. They are often very people-oriented, and desire above everything else to maintain the relationship.

The key word that can be used to describe a Teddy Bear is ACCOMMODATION. Like appreciated people in the service industries, they are willing to accommodate other people, especially their customers.

When conflict arises, a Teddy Bear will often deny that it even exists. When such denial no longer works, they many times will take the blame to end the tension — after all, "the customer is always right!" They see themselves as the one that must pay the price to maintain some sense of relationship. If the Turtle basically said, "No way" to a conflict situation, then the Teddy Bear would respond by saying, "Well, OK, we'll do it your way." On our two-tension graph, this critter lands in the HIGH-LOW quadrant, HIGH in relationships/love and LOW in goals/truth.

Teddy Bears yield to others and lose their goals. Interestingly, this style of dealing with conflict is often held up to be the most Christ-like response. Heeding Jesus' words about going the extra mile or turning the other cheek, these folks commonly think that they are being loving and gracious. They see their accommodation as a living out of the Judgment of Charity. And sometimes it is. But, as we will see when we track the long-term effects of the styles, there is a better way than always choosing to be a Teddy Bear.

POP QUIZ:

What is the key word that describes a Teddy Bear's way of dealing with conflict?

SHARKS

COMPETITION. That's how Sharks see most conflicts. There will be winners and losers. They intend to be on the winning side. They focus more on their goals or understanding of the truth, than on the relationship or love.

If Teddy Bears are extremely people-oriented, the Sharks among us are at the other end of the spectrum. They are very task-focused. These are the folks who get things done. Often found at the top of the business world's food chain, Sharks like to be in control. The key word when conflict arises for a shark is COMPETITION. They see conflict as a battle. The question is who will win and who will lose. Believing that their view is the best means that they should do what they can to win.

Sharks tend to be seen by others as domineering and pushy. Yet they often see themselves as people who are willing to do what needs to be done for the sake of the task at hand. Because their goals are so important to them, this category of conflict manager many times considers that persuasion, power plays, and even coercion are legitimate means to get to their highly valued ends. These actions are seen as OK as long as they get the desired results. There can be a wide variety of sharks, ranging from iron-fisted autocrats to benevolent dictators.

While Turtles are saying, "No way," and Teddy Bears are accommodating with "Your way," the Shark raises his fin and says, "MY WAY!" Therefore, on our two-tension graph the Shark is the opposite of the Teddy Bear. She gets a LOW-HIGH quadrant to live in, LOW in relationships/love and HIGH in goals/truth.

POP QUIZ:

What word best summarizes how a Shark sees conflict?

89

FOXES

NEGOTIATION. That's how Foxes face conflict. Let's compromise and both win-a-little and lose-a-little.

When one has been to the conflict zoo and seen the one-sidedness of the Teddy Bears and the Sharks (the Turtle was nowhere to be seen), it is easy to mistake the Fox as being the most effective style to use for conflict resolution. After all, Foxes do value truth and love. They want to get their goals achieved but they also want to maintain a relationship with you. What could be better?

But before we run too quickly to making the Fox our mascot of choice we need to see where he is placed on the two-tension graph. He is not a HIGH-HIGH but rather a MEDIUM-MEDIUM. While he places some value on relationships, he does not value them as highly as Teddy Bears do. Nor does he go after goals like a Shark does. Rather, he is known by the key word of COMPROMISE.

Words that describe this style include negotiation, conciliation, bargaining, win a little & lose a little, assertive but flexible. Foxes tend to think most forms of persuasion are fine and may even at times fall into the trap of manipulating others. The greatest frustration that people feel with a Fox is rooted in their lack of openness. You usually do not really know what a Fox's agenda is. Even the nature of your relationship with him may be a bit foggy.

This style is the one we see used in the sale and purchase of homes and used cars. People tend to ask a higher figure than they are willing to settle for. Otherwise there is no room for negotiation. This give and take may be the best way to arrive at the market value of an item, but most of us realize that it is not the way to build strong relationships. When my brother-in-law sold me his car several years ago, he did not want to negotiate. Rather, he found out what he would have gotten

 for the vehicle as a trade-in. He then offered it to me for that price. Not only was he willing to give me that great deal, he was willing to guarantee any repairs for the first year. Wow! You may think that this guy must be a Teddy Bear. But he can be quite assertive. Yet, he was not willing to go through the foxy routine because he did not want to endanger our relationship.

POP QUIZ:

What one word summarizes how a Fox tends to see conflict situations?

OWLS

COLLABORATION. Only the Owl style seeks to work together with the other party to find the best solution for all. They want to speak the truth in love and want to help others do the same. They seek, whenever possible, to find a win-win solution for all.

The style that holds out the greatest hope for long-term relationships is the wise Owl. A friend who took this material and taught it in Haiti said that the owl did not fit the local people's experience or knowledge. There the best style was labeled a parrot. A counselor who used this material with at-risk teenagers said that they wanted a more powerful image for this style. The teens liked an eagle (which could work since the eagle used as a symbol for America has both arrows for war and an olive branch for peace — possible emblems of truth and love).

Though other mascots may fit better in certain settings, let us not give up on the Owl too quickly. As one who seeks heavenly wisdom, this traditional symbol of wisdom in America seems to fit quite well. Consider what heavenly wisdom is and see if you do not agree.

Who is wise and understanding among you? Let him show it by his good life, by deeds done in the humility that comes from wisdom. But if you harbor bitter envy and selfish ambition in your hearts, do not boast about it or deny the truth. Such "wisdom" does not come down from heaven but is earthly, unspiritual, of the devil. For where you have envy and selfish ambition, there you find disorder and every evil practice. But the wisdom that comes from heaven is first of all pure; then peace-loving, considerate, submissive, full of mercy and good fruit, impartial and sincere. Peacemakers who sow in peace raise a harvest of righteousness. (James 3:13-17)

"Peacemakers who sow in peace" is the hope of all strong Owls. On the two-tension graph this style comes in as HIGH-HIGH, caring for both the relationships and the goals. They see conflict as an opportunity for COLLABORATION. By highly valuing the relationship and highly valuing their goals, they hope and work for a win-win solution. They put effort toward getting everyone actively involved in a dynamic that could be called synergistic ("1 + 1 = 3", which does not work in math but does in some chemical reactions and biological relationships).

The Owl seeks an open relationship that works towards the best possible solution for everyone. That does not mean that they want to please everyone (that would be a Teddy Bear). Rather, they humbly acknowledge that others, even critics, can have very important insights and perspectives. These may be helpful in creating solutions to the conflict. Owls usually are willing to suspend judgment to investigate all possible avenues of action. They do not drift into the land of "tolerance," where everyone is right. But they will live with uncertainty and "gray" until the issue has been deeply explored.

> **POP QUIZ:**
>
> What one word captures the Owl style?

	ASSESSING MY CONFLICT STYLES	Consistently	Very Often	Often	Occasionally	Rarely	
	Read the descriptions below and then rate how often it is true of you. **Our styles change depending on who we are dealing with. It may be helpful to consider just one relationship or category of role, such as family or work.** **The next page will help you score the assessment.**						
	DESCRIPTION	**1**	**2**	**3**	**4**	**5**	
A	When I disagree with someone, I get energized to compete with them for "the win."						A
B	I like the process of haggling out a fair price for something or for a resolution to a conflict.						B
C	I stay away from conflict by keeping any concerns I have to myself and by backing away from the situation.						C
D	I don't give in easily but firmly defend my side of the issue.						D
E	I press to understand what the other side(s) in a conflict really want, so that we have all the puzzle pieces on the table to work with.						E
F	I would rather walk on eggshells around someone than bring up a point of disagreement.						F
G	I often feel like it's all up to me to fix things by being quiet and putting everyone else's opinions ahead of my own.						G
H	I want to be gentle and yet firm at the same time, trying to express my point of view graciously and yet with full vigor. I want others to do the same.						H
I	I really dislike disagreements or conflicts and will do almost anything to get them resolved, often at the expense of my opinions or desires.						I
J	I make sure others know the strong points of my position on disputed decisions that need to be made.						J
K	I think if you just ignore most conflicts that they just kind-of go away by themselves.						K
L	I tend to keep my thoughts and feelings to myself so that I can have more room to maneuver to a good outcome.						L
M	I believe the truth about an issue is very important and needs to be forcefully stated, even if it incidentally hurts others' feelings.						M
N	I believe there are often solutions available. We need to hear out all sides. Conflict isn't in itself bad. It is an opportunity to clarify for the greater good.						N
O	While I care about what I want, I care more about maintaining peace in my relationship with other people.						O
P	I don't usually tell people what I think about issues in a conflict, but I quietly vote with my feet and avoid conflicts and people I see as "conflict makers."						P
Q	I try to meet people halfway, negotiating my way to a compromise that considers at least some of my goals.						Q
R	I like the process of clarifying, from all points of view, what are the major and minor issues in a conflict, so that we can work together toward a mutual solution.						R
S	I usually think the best we'll do in a serious disagreement is to have both sides give in and meet somewhere in the middle.						S
T	I try to act out of love and am willing to let others win – this is almost always true in the area of preferences and often true in more critical issues.						T

SCORING YOUR CONFLICT STYLES ASSESSMENT

Transfer the scores (1-5) that you gave to each of the descriptions on the previous page. Enter the score next to the identifying letter for the description.				TOTAL the four scores	The lower the score, the more you tend to use this style. Remember, your second and third styles often come out as tension increases.
C	F	K	P	➡	**TURTLE (Avoiding)**
G	I	O	T	➡	**TEDDY BEAR (Accommodating)**
A	D	J	M	➡	**SHARK (Competing)**
B	L	Q	S	➡	**FOX (Negotiating)**
E	H	N	R	➡	**OWL (Collaborating)**

Reflection Notes on the assessment:

As you have understood the styles, do you think the assessment was accurate or not? How so?

Why would it help raise the accuracy by focusing on one relationship or category of role?

It can be very helpful to ask the person(s) you are in interacting with to complete a copy, thinking not of themselves but rather how they perceive you. If you can do that, why do you think there will probably be differences between your scores?

WHAT WE CONTROL MOST IN CONFLICT

We cannot control other people. What we have the most control over is our own motives and methods. If we fight with the Judgment of Charity and seek to operate in an Owl style, we have the greatest opportunity to _influence_ others to do the same.

Since we do not control others, we must remember that our chosen style of conflict management is what we can change and thereby <u>influence</u> others. As we review the five styles, consider the impact that each style can have on others. Of course, there are exceptions and people may try to respond using a variety of styles at different times.

- If I am consistently a Turtle, others will be forced into making decisions for me (or at least without me). Thus, others would be nudged toward the Shark style.

- Likewise, the Teddy Bear pushes people toward Shark-ness — because real life involves day-to-day choices about goals and priorities.

- The Sharks among us (though they usually swim alone) will crush people into a submissive Teddy Bear or hibernating Turtle mode.

- Foxes beget foxes and over the longer course they may give birth to more destructive critters.

- What is clear is this: No style <u>promotes</u> the response of an Owl style EXCEPT the Owl style itself.

.

POP QUIZ:

"When we consistently respond like Teddy Bears or Turtles, what style are we inadvertently promoting in others?"

THE TROUBLE WITH TURTLES

<u>AVOIDING</u> conflict is how turtles deal with problems. There are some problems that are not worth dealing with. Yet, in the long-term, the Turtle <u>undermines relationships by abdicating their goals and not being actively involved</u> in implementing solutions.

Over time the Turtle may become resentful and angry, at either themselves or other folks (or both). They may reach a breaking point and explode, going "postal" to the surprise of all who thought they knew them.

Is there a time to AVOID conflict? Yes, when there is little hope for resolution or the issues are trivial. If someone pulls a gun on you, it is time to give them the trivial stuff in your wallet and hide. It is just not worth it to use any other style. But what happens in the long-term?

Over time Turtles tend to feel marginalized, pushed to the edge of the page and not very important. They sense they are just taking up space. They feel very alone since their withdrawal makes a meaningful relationship virtually impossible. They sometimes change styles because they yearn for a relationship. But then they get hurt or disappointed (as happens in ALL relationships) and they retreat to their familiar shells. The hurt only confirms to them the wisdom of keeping their heads down.

Unless the Turtle has slipped into a deep depression (and has given up on any pursuit of all goals), they tend to become more and more angry that people do not seem to care what they think or want. Their self-talk, which far exceeds their interaction with others, causes them to self-validate their perspectives. This often causes a spiraling inward and downward.

The Turtle who has repressed such feelings can explode suddenly. The sudden Shark-likeness is unexpected to most. But what about the people around a Turtle? It is hard to blame them for responding like Sharks or Foxes. It is so hard to engage the Turtle in seeking a solution (which would be required to practice the Owl style). It becomes easier to just make the decisions needed without them. Sometimes it is not just easier, it is the only way to go. When a choice must be made (and most serious choices do not have unlimited time-frames), it is very difficult to wait out a Turtle.

People can also feel threatened by Turtles. Because a Turtle pulls within themselves, the folks around them must guess what they are thinking. When you make people guess long enough, they almost always guess negatively. In other words, it is very difficult to continue to give the Judgment of Charity when there is no feedback. Recently I heard it put this way, "In the absence of information, people tend to connect the dots in the most pathological way possible." And since Turtles make people guess a lot, they are often seen as arrogant, aloof, uncaring, and self-centered. That is the way the dots seem to line up.

POP QUIZ:

Why is the Turtle style not the best choice in the long-term?

THE TROUBLE WITH TEDDY BEARS

ACCOMMODATING others' goals is how Teddy Bears deal with problems. This style, that emphasizes love over truth, seems very godly. But, in the long-term, Teddy Bears can carry a lot of the responsibility for the failure of relationships. By giving in they tend to promote a Shark style in others, with others believing they are entitled to get their way. When Teddy Bears finally "explode" and pour out all the injustices they have gathered, they tend to blame others and excuse themselves for having enabled others.

Is there a time to choose intentionally to act like a Teddy Bear? Sure. Sometimes we care a lot more about the relationship than we do some little goal. This is true when the goal is a whole lot more important to the other people than it is to us.

When you see the person you are dealing with as very emotionally fragile. When they are not ready to work through the conflict. Then it certainly would be more Christ-like to ACCOMMODATE them. Even as I write this I vacillate. Some Teddy Bears see most people as so needy that they feel they must give in and take the full weight of the relationship on themselves. This tendency to enable others in their weaknesses must be seen for what it is — our mixed-up need to be needed. This potential confusion regarding even our own motives forces us into a greater dependence on God.

So, what happens "inside" a Teddy Bear over time? This person is seen as so loving and kind — someone willing to bend over backwards for others. But what does all that bending feel like? As with the Turtle, Teddy Bears often start to feel used and abused. Perhaps they feel it even more acutely since they do engage in the relationship (whereas the Turtle disengages). They will usually begin to complain that they are the one who always must go first. They wonder if anyone would "take them home from the fair" if they did not do exactly what was expected of them as a stuffed animal.

When the brewing conflict finally erupts, the Teddy Bear often presents themselves as completely innocent. They remember all the times they gave in or gave up what they wanted for the sake of the relationship. They cannot believe the others around them who are surprised by the sudden shift in styles. You see, in time, the Teddy Bear usually rips open its fuzzy little chest and out comes a horror movie version of Jaws. As with the Turtle, Teddy Bears often go "postal."

Being around Teddy Bears can be so frustrating, especially when you want to go out to eat. "Where do you want to go?" The answer always seems to be, "It doesn't matter, whatever you want will be fine." But if you choose incorrectly, the "whatever" is not so fine and the gamesmanship of relationships gets confusing and frustrating. Many people in relationship with a Teddy Bear assume that their way is the best way and that their ideas are the final word. The sense of empowerment can lead to not even checking with the Teddy Bear since they usually "don't care" anyway. This makes for even more Shark-like behavior on the part of those around the Teddy Bear.

POP QUIZ:

Why do many Teddy Bears see themselves as martyrs when the conflict is confronted?

THE TROUBLE WITH SHARKS

COMPETITION. That's how Sharks see most conflicts. This win-lose mentality can result in the Shark swimming alone. This style tends to <u>encourage others to hide</u> as Turtles or Teddy Bears, <u>or to come out fighting</u> as another Shark.

As Sharks press on to get the tasks done, they see conflict as a COMPETITION that must be won. That means that there will always be winners and losers, and they are not planning on being among the losers!

These often-productive people (in the short run) hit some serious problems as time goes on.

That does not mean there is not a time to consciously choose to be a Shark. Sometimes there are enormous time pressures and a quick, vital decision is needed right now. Or perhaps the course of action is very unpopular but is desperately needed. Consider if you were in a church worship service. If there was a fire would you want to call a committee meeting? Would it be most important to you right then to have your feelings considered? Or would you want and expect some loving Shark to stand up and give clear orders (not suggestions) that would lead to everyone making it out alive? Yes, there are moments when we all want a wise, forceful Shark around. But not always!

Within themselves Sharks often wonder why leadership is so lonely. It is easy to assume that others are intimidated by their wisdom or prowess (when it often is just the Shark's teeth that others are wary of). They cannot understand why others are not as committed as they are to the cause at hand. They feel the pressure of decisions and responsibilities. They often feel like getting the job done is all up to them (Teddy Bears often sense the relationship is all up to them). At times they feel like making the right decisions is all up to them. This heads them in the direction of sensing they are entitled to such power. This, in turn, leads to a pride that often does not consider all the facts. And that leads to poor decisions.

I have watched as missionaries on the field get told by others around them that they come across as huge Sharks. After having been given the definitions, these followers of Christ are initially devastated and then defensive. They are sure that they are loving, compassionate, kind, and thoughtful. They do listen and consider the views and ideas of others — or at least that is what their filters are picking up. As we explore why others might see them as so domineering, we find out that what the Shark took for faithful followers were really scared Teddy Bears and Turtles.

A strong Shark makes others feel afraid. Even a moderate Shark learns that the pond is too small for two Sharks, so they morph into some other creature when a bigger Shark is cruising their waters. Often those around a Shark will give verbal assent to the sharp-toothed solutions. But then the nod of the head will become passive-aggressive by not really working hard at implementing those solutions. After all, it was the Shark's idea so "they can make it work!" An

> **POP QUIZ:**
>
> Why does a Shark style hinder the development of healthy long-term relationships?

THE TROUBLE WITH FOXES

NEGOTIATION. Because negotiation only works when we keep secret what our agenda really is, this style <u>tends to erode trust</u> over time. People around a Fox wonder what they really would settle for. Foxes also tend to look at others through the same filters as they use.

explosive Shark will make most people "walk on eggshells," avoiding anything that could set off the monster of the deep.

For many people the Fox's COMPROMISE between the relationship and their goals makes this style the one they default to. Often this style should be chosen when there are time pressures and when a "standoff" (or delay in action) will have serious negative results. Sometimes this is the fastest way to resolve a conflict in which neither party has very strong attachment to their specific goals.

But in the long run, Foxes subtly start to impose on others their own filters. In other words, because we are looking at others' motives in a Foxy way, certainly they are looking at ours in the same way. Foxes often act with hidden agendas seeking to finagle or scheme circumstances to their liking. Thus, they tend to believe that everyone else acts out of the same motives (remember the judgmental posturing of the Pharisees in chapter one). This usually encourages them to be even sneakier and more defensive in their relationships.

The lack of trust that other people feel around them often makes the Fox feel isolated and antagonistic. It is difficult to remain the Fox in the long run. Usually our long-tailed friend will slip into either accommodating others (out of a deep desire for a relationship) or of slipping into a competitive mode (out of perceived competition for goals).

This style is the one we see used in the sale and purchase of homes and used cars. People tend to ask a higher figure than they are willing to settle for. Otherwise there is no room for negotiation. This give and take may be the best way to arrive at the market value of an item, but most of us realize that it is not the way to build strong relationships.

POP QUIZ:

Why is a Fox style ineffective for long-term, deeper, meaningful relationships?

THE BENEFITS OF OWLS

The Owl style holds the greatest promise for developing long-term relationships that are known for both grace and truth.

If we want to be peacemakers and so be called the children of God (see Matthew 5:9), then we must count the long-term costs of our old styles of dealing with conflict. We must ask God to help us want to choose and then to actively engage the Owl style. Only this mode of handling conflict lives out the value of speaking the truth in love, being full of grace and truth.

Sharks may have the truth-part right. And Teddy Bears excel at the love component. But only the Owl will not let go of either one. If we are going to begin to experience true unity, neither of these two tension points is negotiable. The so-called unity of Teddy Bears is a lot of warm fuzz covering up shredded internal tensions. And a Shark's version is really the cowering of the frightened before a dictator. As for Foxes, it becomes an uneasy mix of trying to read the others around them, building alliances, and then voting out of the game those that pose the biggest threat.

Speaking the truth in love will never make reality television. It is just not "exciting" enough. It is like teaching children a new game that uses a deck of cards. We usually begin by having a few "open hands." As everyone lays all their cards on the table we can instruct the kids on what would be the best moves and how the rules of the game work. That is fine for when we are teaching the game. But most of us do not play that way all the time. There is no competition in it. No fun. But marriages, families, and churches are not games.

While not juicy and cut-throat, speaking the truth in love is a wonderful way to experience peace in our relationships. We can build others up without flattery. We can deal with the real issues at hand. The Apostle Paul models what he teaches in many of his letters. No one would consider him a push-over. He has the strength of a Shark to deal with the divisive and thorny issues that faced the churches of the first century. But he almost always frames the truth with a powerful dose of love.

The letter to the Ephesians is a great example. When you carefully study the six chapters, you find that the first three are vitally affirming and useful for filling up the reader with the deep sense of the love of God. These early chapters tell us of God's work and all that He has done for us. Then a transition occurs at the beginning of chapter four. Paul says, considering this calling of God, now we need to live in accordance with it. Practical truth on how to live in the daily issues of life fill the last three chapters. The message of love paves the way for the message of truth. The Owl style holds the greatest promise for those who pursue peace.

> **POP QUIZ:**
>
> How does the Owl style manifest the strengths of the other styles?

"MELT-MOLD-MAKE FIRM"

Using the imagery of making a candle, we can remember that the tools of conflict resolution begin with **MELTING** the wax by giving and expressing the Judgment of Charity, especially about others' motives.

Then we **MOLD** the softened wax by focusing on the truth of the methods that need to change.

The final step is to **MAKE FIRM** the now molded wax. This is done by expecting accountability for the agreed upon changes in the methods we will use in the future.

MELTING is about using the strength of a Teddy Bear and softening hearts through love. Stirring up the Judgment of Charity within us will help us be more gentle and gracious in our methods. We will work hard to help the other party feel more secure and less vulnerable. We will use the least threat level possible, going one-on-one first.

MOLDING using the strength of the Shark and deals with the issue by focusing on truth. Molding the wax is about finding great solutions. This always begins by knowing what the right question really is. After the clarified issue is made the focus of all the parties, then we have to generate as much information as we can toward a solution.

MAKING FIRM is about clarifying and then confirming the action steps all will take to work toward continued peace in the relationship. It is often helpful to write these down and even create track points to make sure they are being applied. This step also includes making sure the process of dealing with future conflict is clear so that we can avoid slipping into the dangerous stage of injustice gathering.

POP QUIZ:

"Why must we MELT before we try to MOLD?"

TWO HANDS OF FORGIVENESS: GOD AND PEOPLE

The Two Hands Model of forgiveness helps us understand how God offers forgiveness to the whole world, but only those who repent and believe are forgiven.

Picture two closed fists. The one fist is up high. It is the hand of God. The lower fist is the one that represents people. The lower hand is balled into a fist to indicate that individual people have sinned. We all have done wrong against God. Therefore, we have closed our fists and withdrawn from the relationship we were created to have with God.

The upper hand becomes a picture of God. The Holy God is described in the Scriptures as a God of wrath, full of righteous indignation and anger. He, too, has His fist clenched toward mankind because of our sin. This leaves us with two clenched fists and a broken relationship.

That is not how we were created. Humankind was made in the image of God for the purpose of a relationship with the Holy Trinity. The image of two hands embracing is a good picture of what it should be like. And it is the picture of what God works to restore through Jesus Christ.

In His grace God offers to us something that we do not deserve — forgiveness. He sent His Son, Jesus, to die on the cross. It was a death that He did not deserve, but one He willingly faced. He took the punishment we deserved. God's anger, His righteous and holy anger, was placed upon Christ through His sacrificial, substitutionary death on our behalf. This is what the Bible calls propitiation. Thus, God's hand, as it were, is opened to the whole world. "God so loved the world that he gave his only Son, that whosoever would believe in him should not perish but have eternal life" (John 3:16).

That does not mean that everyone is forgiven. God has made us individuals with choice and freedom. He gave us the freedom to sin against Him, and He gives us the freedom to accept by faith what He has offered to us as a free gift through Jesus Christ.

The Bible declares that the way to receive that gift offered by God's open hand is to open our hand in repentance and faith. Repentance and faith are the flip sides of the same coin. One cannot truly believe in and trust what Jesus has done without repenting - that is turning away in our hearts from our evil acts and the things that we have done wrong. When an individual repents and believes, his hand is opened towards God's hand. The two hands now come together, "hand-in-hand," a picture of reconciliation.

POP QUIZ:

"Has God forgiven everyone or made a way possible for all to be forgiven?"

TWO HANDS OF FORGIVENESS: DIAGRAMMED

The Two Hands Model of forgiveness helps us understand how God offers forgiveness to the whole world, but only those who repent and believe are forgiven. The goal is completed forgiveness, also called reconciliation.

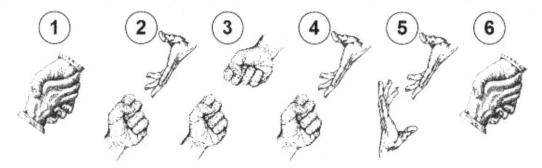

THE TWO HANDS OF FORGIVENESS

1. We were created to have fellowship with our Creator.

2. But we chose to sin and rebel against God (shaking our fist at Him).

3. And the Holy Perfect God was righteously angry with us for our rebellion. He closed His fist in judgment of our sin.

4. But God so loved us that He extended forgiveness (opening His hand) to the whole world through the work of His Son, Jesus. Yet that does not mean that the whole world is forgiven. God honors us by giving us a choice. We must respond in order to be forgiven.

5. We open our hand to receive God's gift by turning away from our sin in repentance and asking for forgiveness, trusting by faith in the work of Jesus.

6. Now the forgiveness is "complete" because we are reconciled to God in restored fellowship with Him as our Creator and Redeemer.

POP QUIZ:

"Why is the model of God's forgiveness the best model for us to use in our dealing with other people?"

TWO HANDS OF FORGIVENESS: APPLIED TO OUR RELATIONSHIPS

The Two Hands Model of forgiveness include "Extended Forgiveness," "Extended Repentance," and "Completed Forgiveness."

"Extended forgiveness" is the same thing God has done through Jesus Christ for the world. He has offered forgiveness to those who are willing to repent and believe. While the offer is presented to the whole world, that does not mean that all are forgiven.

God has opened His hand, as it were, to the whole world. In the same way, on the horizontal (human to human) plane, when we extend forgiveness to someone else, we express a willingness on our part to let go of the bitterness and anger and wrath that burns within us. We are willing to seek reconciliation with another person. BUT, that does not mean that we reduce the dignity of the individual by pretending that their actions do not matter. Though our hand is open we will not pretend there is reconciliation (a joining of the hands) unless they open their fists.

That leads us to the second phase of forgiveness. This is what could be labeled "EXTENDED REPENTANCE." The term extended is used to bring symmetry to the concept of extended forgiveness. This takes place when an individual has realized that they have done wrong and they humbly approach someone else. They offer their hand to them and say, "I am sorry for what I have done, will you please forgive me?"

The same thing is true for extended repentance as was for extended forgiveness — we do not control the other party. Previously, we could not force them to repent. And now we cannot force them to forgive us. Yet, God calls us to extend the hand of repentance when we have done wrong to someone. Another person's wrong responses do not justify us harboring bitterness nor harboring sin. We must be willing to open our hands.

Understanding the two phases of forgiveness helps us in the practicalities of relationships. We can look at the components in the form of a math equation:

EXTENDED FORGIVENESS + EXTENDED REPENTANCE = HAND-IN-HAND FORGIVENESS

The third variable is really the sum of the first two. If, through the grace of God, there is extended forgiveness AND extended repentance, then we have the third phase that can be labeled "HAND-IN-HAND FORGIVENESS." Completed forgiveness is the joyful thing that is spoken about in Romans 5:1-11. It is the reconciliation of people that have been brought back together, one with another. This must always be our ultimate aim and hope. Remember, the process of this "hand-in-hand forgiveness" may take time for the rebuilding of trust.

POP QUIZ:

"Whose 'hand' do we control?"

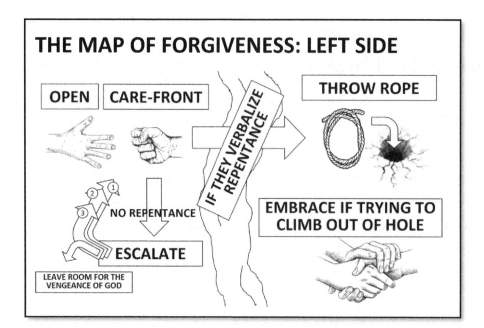

THE MAP OF FORGIVENESS: LEFT SIDE

OPEN   CARE-FRONT   THROW ROPE

IF THEY VERBALIZE REPENTANCE

NO REPENTANCE

ESCALATE   EMBRACE IF TRYING TO CLIMB OUT OF HOLE

LEAVE ROOM FOR THE VENGEANCE OF GOD

SCRIPTURE REFERENCES:
[1] *Matthew 7:1-5*
[2] *Luke 7:36-50*
[3] *Ephesians 4:31-5:2*
[4] *Matthew 18:15-17*
[5] *1 Corinthians 6:1-8*
[6] *Romans 12:14-21*
[7] *1 Peter 2: 22-23*

BEFORE THERE IS REPENTANCE *(Left side of map)*
• We are on the left side of the map, not having crossed the river of repentance.
• We must invite someone to repent, getting in the boat and crossing the river with us.
• We cannot force someone to repent. If they do not repent, they remain on the left side of the river. We can live with an "OPEN HAND TO ALL," but they are not "forgiven" in the sense that their debt is paid. We are NOT "HAND-IN-HAND" with them (on the right side of the river).

DECIDE TO EXTEND AN OPEN HAND
•First, take the log out of our own eye by self-examination.[1]
•Then, put in the love by remembering how much we've been forgiven.[2]
•Prayerfully ask the Spirit to help you forgive as you have been forgiven.[3]

EXTEND AN OPEN HAND BY CARE-FRONTING THE SIN
•It is not enough to "open our hands" in our hearts. We must care enough to confront.
• Take the least threatening posture first (one-on-one).[4]

IF NECESSARY, ESCALATE THE CARE-FRONTING
•Be willing to escalate the conflict out of concern for the other's soul.[4]
•(For professing believers) The final step of escalation is to have the church objectively decide if (1) the other party won't repent and is acting like an unbeliever, (2) the conflict is not over a sin issue but a judgment call or a miscommunication, or (3) the facts cannot be clearly substantiated and the church is to make a decision on the future course of action for the sake of unity.[5] Submit to their judgment.
•(For those not professing faith in Christ) Escalate the conflict as possible, moving up to those to whom the erring party is accountable (boss, principal, police, etc.).

DECIDE TO EXTEND AN OPEN HAND
•Turn the other person over to God for judgment.[6]
•Choose to love your enemies[7] while maintaining wise boundaries that will keep you from unnecessary abuse.

POP QUIZ:

"Can we live "Open Hand to All" but not be reconciled to all?"

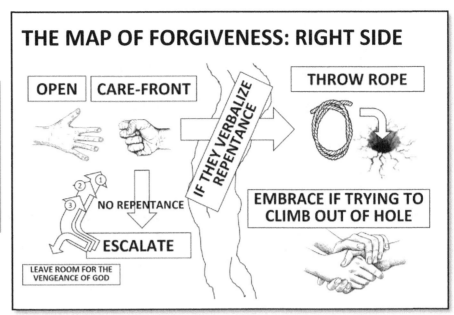

THE MAP OF FORGIVENESS: RIGHT SIDE

OPEN | CARE-FRONT | THROW ROPE

IF THEY VERBALIZE REPENTANCE

NO REPENTANCE

ESCALATE

LEAVE ROOM FOR THE VENGEANCE OF GOD

EMBRACE IF TRYING TO CLIMB OUT OF HOLE

SCRIPTURE REFERENCES:
[8] *Luke 17:3-4*
[9] *1 Corinthians 13:4-8*
[10] *Galatians 6:1-6*
[11] *Ephesians 4:26-27*
[12] *See how God's forgiveness leaves us rejoicing in Romans 5:1-11*

AFTER THERE IS VERBALIZED REPENTANCE *(Right side of map)*

• The other party expresses that they are turning from their sin and desire to be forgiven.

• They have accepted our invitation to "get in the boat and cross the river." We are now moving to the right side of the map.

MAKE THE *DECISION* TO FORGIVE

•As an act of the will, in response to the other party's verbal commitment to repent (and their act of restitution, if possible).8

•This decision includes seeking to restore the Judgment of Charity*, choosing to now look at the others' motives with love, and in the best possible light.[9]

WORK THROUGH THE *PROCESS* OF FORGIVENESS

•Throw a rope down the hole, giving the party, who said they repented, a chance to show that they really have. They will either work hard to climb out of the hole or "hang themselves" and show that they really are still on the left side of the river.

• Using the Judgment of Charity, actively hope for and look for the fruits of repentance (rather than the failures). Affirm the positive.

•Hold the other party responsible for their present actions (failures), without immediately assuming that those actions are evidence that the repentance was not real.

•Keep short accounts of the minor issues. Bear up with the irritants but hold them responsible for the sin issues.[10]

•Do not let the sun go down on your anger. Deal with today's issue while it is still today.[11]

REJOICE IN COMPLETED FORGIVENESS (RECONCILIATION)

•The emotional process is complete when full trust is restored.

•One finds oneself rejoicing in the reconciliation without "actively trying to do so."

•We rejoice in the other person's successes.

•We assume the best motives when a circumstance of "suffering" happens between us and the other party.[12]

POP QUIZ:

"What are some evidences that the process of forgiveness is nearing completion?"

105

FORGIVENESS: A DECISION AND A PROCESS

Forgiveness is a **decision** of the will release someone from their debt by paying the price they owe on their behalf. It is also a **process** of healing that takes time as the reconciliation of "hand-in-hand" peace is sought.

The **decision** is based on the other party's statement that they have repented. The **process** requires the manifestation of the repentant party's visible fruits of repentance. These fruits are what help rebuild trust over time.

Forgiveness that has its hopes set on reconciliation is not an easy, quick-fix. It is initiated with an open hand of grace. Hopefully, it is received by a humble hand of repentance. The decision is then made to forgive and bear the costs of the wrongs done against us.

Many think the relationship will instantly be returned to wholeness. This is almost never true of extended conflict that has finally been care-fronted. In addition to the decision of forgiveness, the process of forgiveness is also needed for such healing to take place.

This process is one of praying and looking at the repentant party through the Judgment of Charity. Specifically, the process will include giving opportunities for the others to manifest the fruits of repentance by "throwing a rope down the hole," so they can climb out of it.

Because of the restored Judgment of Charity, we will not immediately scuttle the peace process because of a small failure on the part of the party who said they repented. We let down the rope in the hopes that they will climb out of the hole, not that they would hang themselves. When we see real effort, even with set-backs, the process of healing continues. But, the Judgment of Charity does not mean that we will not expect accountability for the changes we agreed to. We WILL care-front that failure quickly and graciously.

Forgiveness, as a decision and a process, helps us reset the cycle of conflict back to the first two stages. These safer stages are where the focus is on the problem, and not prosecuting the person. This helps us to lovingly <u>not</u> add up a record of wrongs but be always hoping and always enduring (see 1 Corinthians 13).

POP QUIZ:

"After an extended time of conflict, why doesn't the decision to forgive immediately rebuild trust?"

"I'm sorry you took it that way," is not a good apology. It puts all the blame on the other person. *"I'm sorry that I let you hurt me for so many years,"* is also a terrible apology. Because of our tendency to give ourselves the Judgment of Charity about our own motives, it is easy to assume we bear no guilt. After all, we did not mean to hurt anyone.

How can we give an apology when we were not intentional and, certainly not, malicious? We begin by accepting our responsibility for our methods, even if we had good or neutral motives. We can honestly say, *"I did not mean to hurt you, but I understand that you felt taken for granted when I did not call. I was insensitive, not looking to your interests. Would you please forgive me for not phoning when I was going to be late?"*

This apology would be even stronger if we asked, "What can I do in the future to make this right or at least not to repeat the same thing?"

POP QUIZ:

"Do we have to have "bad motives" to be responsible
for "bad methods?"

Numerous books written by Christian counselors will advocate that we can forgive without ever care-fronting the other person. They say forgiving someone who has sinned against us sets us free. We no longer need to be a prisoner of the wounds they inflicted. Some books even suggest that God has already forgiven all people and that He no longer condemns anyone. Yes, they usually admit that not everyone has appropriated this forgiveness, but their message remains confusing.

If God no longer condemns then how will Jesus judge people and send those who are not forgiven through His blood to an eternity in hell? If God has released all from the debt of their trespasses, then why would any face His judgment?

A better tool for the counselor's toolbox is the teaching found in the Old Testament and in Romans 12:18-21. We can find emotional release and psychological freedom not by pretending non-repentant people are forgiven. But, by entrusting them to God by leaving room for His vengeance.

The Scriptures are full of promises that God will judge our enemies. He will make all things right in the end. All sin will be paid for. Either people will repent and believe in Jesus, with God the Son making full payment for their debt. Or, non-repentant people will bear the eternal cost of sinning against a holy God.

Those folks who have hurt us and for whom there is no opportunity to care-front, we do not forgive them. We open our hands and entrust them into the hands of God, leaving room for His vengeance.

What about those enemies that we do have contact with, who we have care-fronted but who will not repent? Romans 12 tells us not to avenge ourselves but to leave it to the wrath of God. And then to choose to do loving acts like feeding them or giving them something to drink.

POP QUIZ:

"Why is leaving room for the vengeance of God not being judgmental on our part?"

THROW THE ROPE DOWN THE HOLE

This phrase captures the idea of graciously giving the person who has verbalized repentance a chance to show that they were genuine.

It also protects the injured party, who has made the decision of forgiveness, from the abuse of those who only mouthed the words of repentance but had no change of heart. This is not about making others "prove they have changed" as we watch them with a critical eye. Rather, it is praying and rooting for them to follow through because we are Christ-followers who pursue peace.

Forgiveness is both a decision and a process. Even before we make the decision to forgive, we open our hands and entrust ultimate judgment to God, extending the hand that offers forgiveness. If the other party repents, receiving our offer, we make the decision to forgive. Then we must seek a way forward, toward hand-in-hand reconciliation or completed forgiveness. Part of the way forward is "throwing the rope down the hole."

The decision of forgiveness does not mean that we do not hold people accountable for their future actions. It is reasonable and biblical to expect that their voiced repentance becomes the visible fruits of repentance. In a sense, to rebuild trust, the other party must climb out of the hole.

A mediator can help a fearful forgiver move into hope by getting the parties to agree on what climbing out of the hole would look like in their situation. Then, with a restored or at least strengthened Judgment of Charity, the forgiver can now pray for and root for the other party to use the rope to climb out of the hole.

This tool also provides the safety of the core commitment of expecting accountability. The party that has voiced repentance may have lied, with the result that they will "hang themselves" on the rope of opportunity. Their gross failure would expose them and then the conflict would be redefined. Instead of being a relationship pursuing peace, it would become one divided by sin. The rope helps make evident that while they <u>spoke</u> of repentance, they have become known by their <u>fruits</u>.

POP QUIZ:

"Why doesn't 'throwing the rope down the hole' usually work if we haven't regained the Judgment of Charity?"

FORGIVENESS QUESTIONS & ANSWERS: Head

Questions of the Head

These are common questions dealing with the application of the biblical teaching on forgiveness. See also the separate "Questions of the Heart."

1) **Is it really sinful to just avoid the other person rather than seeking reconciliation?**
   Especially in the body of Christ, the Church, it is. We are given commands to live in harmony with each other. Many of the forgiveness commands focus on our relationship with a "brother."

2) **Are the commands about forgiveness just for other Christians ("brothers")?**
   Even as we are told to do good to everyone, but especially the household of faith. So, we are to offer forgiveness to all, but there is a special urgency for those who claim to be "in Christ" since our unity is to be part of a convincing testimony to a cynical world.

3) **Do I just forgive, even though she won't admit she did anything wrong?**
   No. You can open your hand but don't act like they have repented in word and action. Be kind but firmly keep your boundaries. Be willing to escalate the conflict as described in Matthew 18:15-17.

4) **They won't admit they did anything wrong or won't repent. Do I not forgive them?**
   In the sense that you "extend forgiveness" you should forgive them. BUT you should escalate the care-fronting until the church declares them unbelievers (or escalate as far as possible). Then leave room for the vengeance of God and love your enemies.

5) **How can the biblical process keep us from falling into enabling another person's sinful actions?**
   By having us "care enough to confront" those who are sinning, we don't allow them to continue in their behavior without understanding the eternal consequences of sinning with "a high hand."

6) **How do I specifically escalate the care-fronting to the level of church discipline?**
   Who you take with you (1 or 2 witnesses) is really up to you. They should be mature believers. They could be elders. If this step doesn't work, then "taking it to the church" begins by telling a pastor or elder that you need to take the care-fronting to the next level. At our church the elders will seek to work toward repentance and reconciliation first. If that is not successful, then the members of the congregation will be informed and asked to decide if the erring person is to be "declared an unbeliever."

7) **How can someone be "loving" and yet be "firmly intolerant" of sinful behavior?**
   We can be loving by opening our hand to ALL. This includes being loving to even our enemies. It does not mean we treat our enemies, or those who are unwilling to repent, as those we are reconciled to (hand-in-hand). Therefore, we are firmly intolerant of their sin.

8) **Do we forgive only if there is repentance or are we called to forgive regardless of the offender's contrition?**
   We OFFER forgiveness to all, but we actually only forgive the repentant. "Open hand to all. Hand-in-hand for repentant."

(Continued next page)

9) Why isn't forgiving the same thing as condoning sin?
Condoning sin happens when we either avoid the person who has sinned against us OR we deal with the conflict by accommodating the others by <u>not</u> holding them responsible for their sin.

10) What are the marks of genuine repentance?
A verbal acknowledgment of what they did wrong and the hurt it caused, followed by a humble request to be forgiven. If possible, generous restitution is offered. Only in time will the fruits of repentance become visible in a changed life. A truly repentant person is profoundly grateful that they are forgiven.

11) How do I evaluate if his words represent genuine repentance or cheap regret or personal manipulation?
In faith we must make the decision to forgive but then allow time to confirm their repentance by manifesting the fruits of change.

12) Can there be forgiveness AND consequences?
After the decision of the will to forgive, we must not punish the other person since we have "paid their debt." But a truly repentant person will understand that they need to show forth the fruits of repentance. Paying someone's debt is not the same as restoring their "assets" (e.g. an adulterer may be forgiven but no longer qualifies to be an elder who is to be a one-woman man).

13) If I forgive my cheating spouse, does that mean that I have to stay married to them?
Sexual immorality is a biblical ground for divorce, but it does not mandate it. Repeated unfaithfulness is evidence of the guilty party not being truly repentant. If the Holy Spirit gives a person freedom to divorce after the one-flesh relationship has been broken (especially repeatedly), they are allowed to do so.

14) Why is the "judgment of charity" so important to the process of forgiveness and the rebuilding of trust?
If our "filters" are clogged with the judgment of bitterness, then we will "find fault" easily with the forgiven party. We must remember that "Love covers a multitude of sins" (1 Pet. 4:8b).

15) Does disciplining our child mean that we are not forgiving them?
We "arouse compassion" and open our hand to our kids, "extending forgiveness." If our goal is a child with a tender and humble heart, we discipline (care-front) toward the end that they repent. We escalate the discipline as needed. And when they repent, we then forgive. The end we seek is a repentant heart.

16) What do I do when I have truly repented, but the other party just won't let it go?
Not forgiving a repentant person is a sin. If the PROCESS of forgiveness is stuck, then it is appropriate to care-front the unforgiving party for their sin.

17) Are forgiveness and reconciliation always connected? Is it possible to have one without the other?
Extended forgiveness, when received by repentance, begins the process of reconciliation. The gold standard of God through Jesus is forgiveness that yields reconciliation that all rejoice in.

18) Do I need to be forgiven for not meeting all of my children's expectations and desires? If not, why do I feel like I do?
Forgiveness is about sin, not unmet expectations and desires. We must learn to distinguish between true guilt and false guilt. It is possible for someone to be "hurt" by an action/inaction but that does not necessarily make the action sinful.

FORGIVENESS QUESTIONS & ANSWERS: Heart

Questions of the Heart

These are common questions dealing with the emotional barriers to applying the biblical teaching on forgiveness. See also the separate "Questions of the Head."

1) **What are the signs of unforgiveness?** (*this list is adapted from Gary Inrig's book, Forgiveness*) *Takes offense easily; caress hurts that sometimes go back years, even to childhood; rehearse the wrongs done to them as if reciting a script; absolutely convinced that they were— and are— victims; so preoccupied with the wrong done to them— which may be and often is severe and painful— that they cannot see the wrong in them, obsessed by their own pain they become oblivious to the pain that they inflict on others; gossiping about the errors in others' lives; talking often of past "hurts;" immediately thinking the worst of another person's motives (little or no "judgment of charity"); hyper-vigilance that is looking and waiting for the other person to mess up.*

2) **Can't I just forgive from my heart and not have to deal with these people again? What's so wrong with that?**
It is not how God forgave us in Christ. If that were what God did, He would "feel" better but we would spend an eternity in hell anyway, separated from Him.

3) **How long do I wait— until I feel able or willing to forgive?**
In faith and obedience, make a decision of the will to open your hand to extend forgiveness and to forgive if they say they repent. "A clean wound can heal."

4) **I am so wounded by shame that I just feel like I can't forgive or that I'm even worthy to be a forgiver. What do I do?**
Forgiveness, both offering and receiving it, is so very hard. For those deeply wounded, it is impossible without the healing touch of Jesus. We must let go of our pride and humbly ask for the healing only He can provide.

5) **Why do I keep feeling like I need to ask for forgiveness, but they are the one who keeps hurting me?**
We must be clear who needs to ask forgiveness. The initial care-fronting is NOT about our anger and bitterness. It IS about their sinful actions. A tender-hearted person can be so hurt by the broken relationship that they are willing to "take the blame" even when it isn't theirs to take.

6) **What do I do when someone says they repent but I really don't believe them?**
Luke 17:3-4 makes clear that we are required to forgive if they say they repent. Even the directive to forgive 7 times in a day makes it clear that there is no evidence of the fruits of repentance yet.

(Continued next page)

112

7) Does my tormentor just get off scot-free, when he's put me through so much?

If we make the other person "pay," then we have not forgiven them. This is not how God in Christ forgives us.

8) Doesn't "opening my hand" expose me to further hurt? Why would I do that?

When we open our hand to another person we do make ourselves vulnerable to further hurt. But a Christ-follower is motivated by God's forgiveness and the hope of being a reflection of His love in our relationships.

9) Does being cautious and not completely trusting mean that I haven't forgiven?

Not necessarily. If you made the DECISION to forgive recently and the PROCESS of forgiveness has been fairly short, we should expect these feelings. Assuming there are no further sinful actions on their part, our prayer needs to be that we "again decide" (an act of the will) that we have forgiven them.

10) What do I do when I know I've forgiven but the bad, bitter, angry feelings come back every once in a while?

During the PROCESS of forgiveness, these feelings will probably come back. These are the "ding-dongs" that Corrie Ten Boom talked about – we aren't pulling the bell's rope anymore, but the clapper still hits once in a while. Assuming there is no "new" sin against us, we must decide again that we have forgiven the other party.

11) Does "being crabby again" mean that I wasn't really repentant the last time I asked forgiveness?

The question really is whether you have gone back and sinned again, doing what you had repented of when you asked forgiveness. Some sins, like being "crabby" will probably need to be repented of numerous times as we learn to walk in the Spirit and manifest His fruit.

12) What am I supposed to do about the "wall of ice" (non-responsiveness) from those I think I should be closer to?

Creating division in the body of Christ is a sin. Care-fronting the sin by graciously bringing up the METHODS of the other party (without immediately judging their MOTIVES) can expose the "hidden" conflict issues so they can be addressed.

13) Can someone really "forgive and forget?"

We can't really forget but we can choose "not to remember" . . . putting the memories in the back of the bottom drawer of our minds. "I distinctly remember forgetting that."

"DO I HAVE TO FORGIVE GOD?"

A common misunderstanding of forgiveness is made evident when someone says that they need to forgive God. God has never and will never sin. He will never be in our debt. We cannot bear the cost of His wrongdoing.

Forgiveness is about sin, not unmet expectations and desires. God has never and will never sin, so it is wrong to speak of "forgiving Him." To do so is to imagine that we are God's judge. As believers, we wait for the return of Christ to make things as they should be. The mess we are in is because of our choices, not God's incompetence or sinfulness.

Using the example of debt, the Bible pictures forgiveness as the choice to bear the cost of the wrong done by another. I owe you money. You choose to forgive me my debt. You have therefore taken the cost of my debt and "paid" it yourself.

With this picture in mind, is it possible to forgive God? Is there any way that He is in debt to us? Can we release Him of any obligation that He owes us? The answer is a definite NO. We cannot forgive God, for God has never sinned.

It is only when we adopt the world's false notion of forgiveness, that we would dare say we should forgive God. This view presents forgiveness as being all about "letting go" of our hurt and anger. Since we can be disappointed that God did not meet our expectations or dreams, we can feel hurt and even anger toward Him. The world would say we let God off the hook and set ourselves free by doing so. But, to say we forgive God is to clearly imply that He has wronged us in some way. We have become His judge.

Far better is to understand that we can and should choose to give God the Judgment of Charity. When we look at the things He has allowed into our lives, that we do not like, through the lens of love, we can continue to trust Him. As Romans 5:1-11 teaches us, we can even rejoice in our sufferings because we KNOW God loves us. The reason "FOR" this is, "For one will scarcely die for a righteous person—though perhaps for a good person one would dare even to die— For while we were still weak, at the right time Christ died for the ungodly. but God shows his love for us in that while we were still sinners, Christ died for us." (Romans 5:6-8).

One could argue that this is what people mean when they say we must forgive God. But, to so distort the meaning of a word is to rob it of its power in the correct context it should be used. To do this sets us up to imagine that our forgiveness of another person is just an emotional "letting go," with no thought toward even seeking possible reconciliation.

> **POP QUIZ:**
>
> "Why is it impossible to forgive God?"

114

"DO I NEED TO FORGIVE MYSELF?"

Often people say that they can't forgive themselves. Is "forgiving ourselves" in line with biblical teaching?

No, it is not. Better would be to say that "I need to accept God's forgiveness." It is good that we see the weight of what we've done wrong. It is bad that we allow the Evil One to condemn us even though Christ has forgiven us.

The idea of forgiving ourselves, while very popular, is not biblical. It is based on a weak, psychologically-driven, anthropocentric definition of forgiveness. This worldly view of forgiveness says we must "let go" both of our anger and hurt toward others and the sense of guilt and shame we feel for our sins.

The Bible DOES give us an answer for dealing with our sin and shame. It is taking God at His word and by faith believing that there is now no condemnation for those who are in Christ (see Romans 8). We must accept by faith what God says He has done for us through the saving work of Jesus. Our continued sense of shame is because we believe the accuser of the brethren rather God.

POP QUIZ:

"Why can we not forgive ourselves, rather needing to accept God's forgiveness and acceptance of us?"

FALSE FORGIVENESS = NO PEACE

The world tells us to forgive for our own sake. We must "let go" of the hatred and anger for our own emotional health. Biblical forgiveness has as its hope and end goal the reconciliation of estranged parties.

We have rejoicing and exulting because of God's forgiveness that has brought peace to our relationship with Him. True, completed forgiveness with a repentant party, should yield the same sort of relational peace. It is this peace that we are pursue.

When the goal of forgiveness is not the seeking of reconciliation when possible, weaker purposes tend to hijack this wonderful blessing. For many, "forgiveness" is something we do when we "let go" of our anger and our desire and commitment to fight for our way. With this lesser purpose in mind, we can say we have forgiven the other party but then take no steps to be reconciled with them.

Reconciliation, or completed forgiveness, is not always possible. But it must remain our hope and prayer as we approach conflict. That is the only way we can forgive as God forgives us. He offers forgiveness to the whole world. All who repent and believing, turning away from their sin and to Christ, will be forgiven. The goal of this gracious offer by the Lord is for us to be brought back, reconciled to Him in a relationship defined by "peace" (see Romans 5:1-11).

When we say we have forgiven but refuse to worship in the same room as the "repentant, forgiven one," we have bought into a false forgiveness. We have traded God's strong forgiveness, the true forgiveness, for a worldly knock-off. As Christ-followers, we must not settle for the division and separation that suggests that perhaps the Father did not send the Son (see John 17:20-21).

POP QUIZ:

"What is the disconnect between declaring, "You are forgiven,"
and, "I never want to see you again?"

```
┌─────────────────────────────┐
│ CHECKLIST:                  │
│ WHEN WE HAVE CONFLICT       │
└─────────────────────────────┘
```

WHEN YOU KNOW THERE'S A PROBLEM . . . BETWEEN <u>YOU</u> AND SOMEONE:

☐ **PRAY** – seek the Lord and ask Him to give all parties tender and humble hearts that are teachable.

☐ **HUMBLE YOURSELF** – as you pray, ask the Lord to help you see whatever motives or methods you may have had that led to or escalated the conflict.

☐ **REFUSE TO GOSSIP** – seek the Spirit's help to NOT go talk to a bunch of other folks, either personally or electronically.

☐ **STIR UP YOUR JUDGMENT OF CHARITY** – in addition to asking the Holy Spirit to keep you away from the sin of gossip, ask Him to help you be more loving.

☐ **OPEN YOURSELF TO REBUKE AND CORRECTION** – before you go talk directly with them, ask God to help you be wise enough to hear what they have to say and to accept responsibility for your part of the mess.

☐ **GO TALK DIRECTLY WITH THEM** – consider what would help you feel open to having a "hard talk," and then offer those things to the other party. In as safe an environment as possible, share your concerns.
  - Begin with sharing that you <u>value them</u> and their friendship. Your hope is to be able to strengthen and restore that relationship.
  - Ask if it would be OK to <u>begin with prayer</u>. In your prayer, review what you have processed with God in the previous steps (humility, love, openness to correction).
  - Share the difference between <u>motives and methods</u>.
  - Let them know that anybody has the right to call a "<u>time out</u>." This would immediately stop the conversation. The only next step would be to agree on who would be able to help in the role of a mediator. It should then be agreed to who would contact the potential mediator, by when, and how they will let the other party know of the plans.

☐ **ASK FOR FORGIVENESS** –
  - Ask them if there are methods, things that you have done, or left undone, that have been part of building the wall between you. Write down the specifics and clarify if needed. If they slide over into talking about your motives, ask the Lord to help you not get defensive.
  - if sins have been pointed out (what you did or left undone), ask forgiveness specifically for them. This is true whether you meant to do them or not
  - End your apology with the question, "Will you forgive me of this?"

(Continued next page)

117

☐ **OFFER TO MAKE THINGS RIGHT** – After apologizing, ask if there is anything that you can do to "make it right." These follow through steps help rebuild trust. <u>Write down</u> these things.

☐ **OFFER FORGIVENESS –**
  o the other party may see, on their own, their need to ask forgiveness. If they do not, graciously tell them that there are some things they did (or left undone) that hurt you as well.
  o Ask if you can now share what you see those issues to be.
  o Share the specific methods that you witnessed that need to be addressed. Try not to address their motives, about which you would be guessing. Ask them if what you shared makes sense. Clarify.
  o Ask them whether they will accept responsibility for their methods.
  o Ask them if they want to ask forgiveness for what they did (or left undone)?
  o Their offer of repentance may not be as specific or direct as yours (see above), but if you believe they are sincerely turning away from their sin, be gracious and receive their offer and forgive them.
  o If there are action steps that you believe would help you rebuild trust, let them know what those action steps would be. These would be acts that would help "make it right."

☐ **CAPTURE THE ACTION STEPS**
  o Write down the action steps that both parties agree to do and the time frame for getting them done.
  o Discuss if there should be another get-together to ensure that something hasn't gone sideways in the reconciliation process. If so, set a date.

☐ **PRAY TOGETHER** – thanking God for the grace to forgive and be forgiven.

☐ **FOLLOW THROUGH ON THE ACTION STEPS AND REBUILD TRUST** – understanding the difference between repentance and the fruits of repentance, we can help rebuild trust by being fruitful and effective in manifesting our repentance in the agreed upon action steps. If specific action steps are not acted upon, care-front the other party using the same principles as taught above.

CHECKLIST:
WHEN OTHERS HAVE CONFLICT

WHEN YOU "KNOW" THERE'S A PROBLEM . . . BETWEEN OTHER PEOPLE:

☐ **PRAY** – seek the Lord and ask Him to give all parties tender and humble hearts that are teachable.

☐ **HUMBLE YOURSELF AS A PEACEMAKER** – as you pray, ask the Lord to help you not elevate yourself to the role of being either a judge, detective, or hit-man. As someone who has information only by hearsay or by inference (inferring a conclusion based on a behavior you saw), it is NOT your job to become the judge of these folks. It is NOT your job to get to the bottom and then present your findings to some judge. It is NOT to become a "hit man" for one of the parties. In humility, ask the Lord to help you be a peacemaker.

☐ **REFUSE TO GOSSIP** – seek the Spirit's help to NOT go talk to a bunch of other folks, either personally or electronically.
   o If you learned about the situation from one of the parties involved, you may have been a party to unintentional gossip. It would NOT be gossip only if the information was shared with you to seek your help to directly go and care-front the situation.
   o If you see that you have participated in gossip by listening to the gossip and not correcting it, repent. You must go to the person who spoke the gossip.

☐ **STIR UP YOUR JUDGMENT OF CHARITY** – in addition to asking the Holy Spirit to keep you away from the sin of gossip, ask Him to help you be more loving.
   o Ask Him to help you "fight," in your mind, for the best possible motives that may lie behind the methods of the other party. Many people gossip unintentionally, seeking to find emotional support or even wisdom as to what they should do next. The problem is, what they need to do is talk directly with the other party, not others.
   o Make sure you are ready to care-front the individuals who have spoken to you about the situation. This includes having a spirit of gentleness and grace.

☐ **GO TALK WITH WHO TALKED WITH YOU** –
   o It is NOT our job to confront others based on hearsay, even if we trust the person from whom we "heard say" the accusations.
   o It IS our duty to talk with the person who talked with us since we are actual "witnesses" of that interaction.
   o Our care-fronting of this person should follow the guidelines for "WHEN YOU KNOW THERE'S A PROBLEM . . . . . . AND IT IS BETWEEN YOU AND SOMEONE."

(Continued next page)

119

☐ **OFFER TO HELP THEM "GO TO THEIR BROTHER" AND HOLD THEM ACCOUNTABLE TO DO SO.**
  o Part of talking with the person who told you about the situation goes beyond stopping their gossip. It moves to helping them do the next right thing, which would be to go and talk directly with the other party.
  o This step ensures that you are not just gossiping. You may be talking "bad" about a person "behind their backs," BUT it is to figure out how to talk with them directly.
  o Specific action steps, that are written down, will help make sure that we do what's right until what is right gets done. Putting dates to these steps will help as well.
  o If the person who talked with you initially says they can now handle it on their own, ask them if you can call them by a certain date to make sure things were followed up as we hoped.

POP QUIZ:

"Why is it so important to stir up our Judgment of Charity before we care-front others on what we think was gossip?"

SINS AND RESENTMENT LISTS: A TOOL

This tool asks both parties in a conflict to wait on God, asking the Holy Spirit to show them their own sins, as well as their hurts and resentments.

These lists are then graciously shared to allow the choice of forgiveness to take place. This is in hopes of restoring the Judgment of Charity and beginning the process of rebuilding trust.

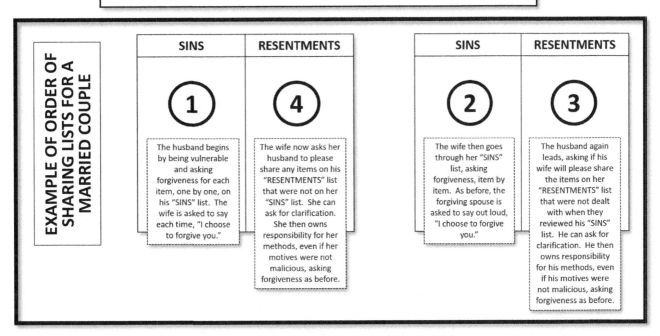

EXAMPLE OF ORDER OF SHARING LISTS FOR A MARRIED COUPLE

SINS	RESENTMENTS
1	**4**
The husband begins by being vulnerable and asking forgiveness for each item, one by one, on his "SINS" list. The wife is asked to say each time, "I choose to forgive you."	The wife now asks her husband to please share any items on his "RESENTMENTS" list that were not on her "SINS" list. She can ask for clarification. She then owns responsibility for her methods, even if her motives were not malicious, asking forgiveness as before.

SINS	RESENTMENTS
2	**3**
The wife then goes through her "SINS" list, asking forgiveness, item by item. As before, the forgiving spouse is asked to say out loud, "I choose to forgive you."	The husband again leads, asking if his wife will please share the items on her "RESENTMENTS" list that were not dealt with when they reviewed his "SINS" list. He can ask for clarification. He then owns responsibility for his methods, even if his motives were not malicious, asking forgiveness as before.

The commitment is made to wait alone on God for one undistracted hour.
1. This time begins by each person asking the Holy Spirit to reveal to them any sins that they have committed against their spouse or other party.
    a. These may be sins of commission or omission.
    b. These sins are written on their "Sins" list.
    c. These items must be specific. General statements like, "I've been unthoughtful" are not as helpful as, "I've was unthoughtful when I did not remember our anniversary."
2. After the point where no additional sins are being brought to mind by the Holy Spirit, the person prays again. This time the request is for help in being honest about the resentments or bitterness they have toward the other person for sins they have committed against them.
    a. Again, these may be sins they have committed, or things left undone (sins of commission OR omission).
    b. These are written on their "Resentments" list.

FOR COMPLETE INSTRUCTIONS: SEE MEDIATION TRIAGE:
3 SESSION TRIAGE INSTRUCTIONS

POP QUIZ:

"Why would we begin by looking at our own sins first?"

"TIME-OUT!"

Facing conflict can feel very chaotic and threatening. By giving the power of a "time-out," all parties can safely indicate that, for them, things are feeling "out of control."

Calling a "time-out" does not stop the process, but rather gives a moment to decide together what would be needed to move forward more effectively. Seeking the help of a mediator, whom all trust, is often a next step. Taking a moment to pray together also makes an enormous difference.

The idea of a "time-out" comes from the crazy moments of a basketball game. Even if we are falling out of bounds, we can stop the game in its tracks. This gives us a chance to regroup and reset our team. The same is true of this simple, but powerful tool in helping us through conflict.

Permission to use a time out is often given by the more assertive party in the relationship. By giving the party that tends to avoid or accommodate in conflict this tool, they are given a way to communicate that their "shields are going up." The more Shark-like person may not be meaning to come across as attacking and perhaps they are not. But, the other party *feels* like they are under attack.

I have suggested to parents and children, as well as to couples, when a time-out is called that everything stops. They then hold hands and each person prays. Asking God to get involved in the conflict usually changes the tone of things tremendously.

It is OK for someone to ask for some time to process things on their own. What is not OK is to use a time-out to avoid dealing with the situation all together. If there is a serious impasse, then it is critical to find the help of a mediator.

POP QUIZ:

"When should someone call a "time-out" in a conflict situation?"

WHY TAKE NOTES?

Immediately after a reconciliation moment, there is a sense of peace and hope. However, if what we remember to be **the follow-up action steps do not occur,** the return of an infection of bitterness readily follows.

Taking notes, and having all parties agree on the notes afterwards, helps us to **remember with "ink"** and not just with our flawed memories.

Notes help us **focus on the methods** of the action steps rather than side-tracking to our perceptions of the other person's motives.

This tool is especially helpful for a mediator but can also be used by anyone in a conflict situation. Even when the hurts have been exposed and forgiveness extended, there is a process of forgiveness as it moves to "hand-in-hand" reconciliation. This time of rebuilding trust is when we are looking for manifestations of the fruits of repentance.

The follow-up steps that are agreed to are those fruits. The wise mediator will have the parties clarify and agree that these fruits will help them give the others the Judgment of Charity. Then it becomes critical to set due dates and track points. These steps are part of the commitment of expecting accountability.

These dates can be tied to what the parties agree to do or stop doing. Often there is also a track point when the mediator agrees to either receive a call or initiate communication to make sure things are on target. To lose all the forward ground because of a lack of follow-up will make facing conflicts in the future even harder.

POP QUIZ:

"Which is stronger: the weakest ink or the strongest memory?" Why?

People who have been hurt often want to withdraw from the relationship. When care-fronted and asked, *"I value our relationship, but have sensed a wall between us. Have I sinned against you in some way?"*, the response may be, *"No, but I just need some time (or space) before I can talk this through."*

The hurt individual may be emotionally fragile at this point. It may be very loving to act like a Teddy Bear and just accommodate their request. But, the wise pursuer of peace may also want to add, *"When would be a good time for me to check with you again."*

Unfortunately, the answer often follows the lines of, *"I don't really know how long it will take. I'll get back with you when I am ready."* We could press for a date to track things, knowing that conflict-avoiders may never think the time is right. However, we cannot force the other party to set a date because we are not responsible for their response. If they remain in the same local fellowship with us, we may be in a position to seek reconciliation with them in the future, even asking others to help mediate.

Folks who avoid dealing with hurt and frustration, and then withdraw to relieve the pain, misunderstand the nature of healing. Separation heals nothing. Relationships cannot be mended if there is no point of contact. Withdrawal is not the pursuit of peace but a self-defensive maneuver. When we have been cut, the doctor cleans the wound. Then she stitches the two sides of the cut together. Leaving the two sides apart for a time will make future healing more difficult, not less.

It can be frustrating when we are for peace and others only want the absence of conflict and pain. Often these folks withdraw from the local body of believers, making it almost impossible to escalate with the help of others. The only course of action is to continue to entrust them to God and pray for them with a Judgment of Charity. Their woundedness and even immaturity may explain their response, but they really are not valid excuses. It remains a sad day for our testimony regarding the glory of Jesus.

> **POP QUIZ:**
>
> "Why is withdrawal not a pursuit of peace?"

HAVE I LOST THE JUDGMENT OF CHARITY?

Everything we do should be done out of love. Even if our methods are right, if our motives are not loving then it all amounts to nothing (see 1 Corinthians 13).

It is easy to fool ourselves about our own hearts. Ask the Holy Spirit to help you examine yourself and to judge yourself, so that you will not needed to be judged.

☐ I keep a **"record of wrongs,"** as evidenced by bringing up a list of things the other person has or has not done? That is, I tend to go "historical" when I get into a conflict with that person.

☐ My **self-talk** about the other party focuses on their motives rather than their methods.

☐ I am **"quick to anger"** when I talk with or about this person.

☐ I often **"pigeon-hole"** them, thinking, "They are just like _____. I guess that's what *"those kind of people"* are like."

☐ I see an increase in my **"mind-reading,"** thinking, *"They ought to 'just know this' by now!"*

☐ I gossip about the other person by **saying negative things about them behind their backs,** even though there is no agenda in that third-party conversation to seek to make things better (such as when you are getting counsel on how to restore the broken or strained relationship).

☐ I **obsess** about another person, thinking, *"if I could just get rid of them,"* that my life would be so much better.

☐ I have **lost hope** that anything is going to change in my relationship with the other person.

☐ When I catch yourself thinking thoughts without the Judgment of Charity about this person (that is, judging the other person's motives with great skepticism and pessimism), I **don't actively try to regain (or "fight for") the Judgment of Charity.**

☐ I have had to **leave** teams, clubs, churches, or even communities because I just can't stand being around some other person.

☐ I rebuff any efforts that they may make to work toward reconciliation, increasingly seeing them as **hypocritical manipulations.**

☐ I have **given up praying positively** for the person who hurt or disappointed me — the one I struggle not to resent for what they did or did not do.

(continued next page)

☐ I would **never reconsider** getting re-married, going back to the same church, joining the team again, or in some way again being in **a tangible, committed relationship** with the person who hurt me (assuming they have sought forgiveness and manifest the fruit of repentance after I care-fronted them).

☐ I am often **judgmental** of the other person's perspective, without even being curious to learn more about how they see things.

☐ I have **lost the sense of freedom** in the relationship, with "walking on egg shells" being par for the course.

☐ I am often **irritated** by the way the other person feels, especially about me.

☐ I am **fixated** and keep thinking about how much I've been hurt, even though the other person has asked for forgiveness and I said that I did forgive them.

☐ I **keep bringing up**, or am tempted to bring up, the "hurtful incident from the past." This may be in defending my actions in discussions with others or in new arguments with the person who hurt me. I may say something like, "This is just like when . . ."

☐ It is difficult for me to make or sustain **eye contact** with the person who hurt me.

☐ I find myself thinking about ways to **avoid** this person.

☐ When this person comes up in a discussion, I find myself **wanting to be "better" than they are**, in a sense competing with them for a "win."

☐ I let myself get to the point of **merely feeling numb**, letting my heart imagine that indifference to the other person is the same thing as forgiveness.

☐ I have a high level of my **"fixed attention"** toward the other person, having an unusual attention to the others' motives in even mundane matters. It is increasingly difficult to take captive every thought (see 2 Corinthians 10:5). Rather than use my sentiments as a springboard to pray for them and our relationship, I seem to march back into the courtroom to engage in more mental prosecution.

GENTLENESS-MEEKNESS ASSESSMENT

Place a check in the column that best reflects how you see yourself. Make a copy of this assessment and ask your spouse or friend to assess you. It could make for a great growth opportunity. Total each column and reflect on your progress in reflecting Christ's character.

	5	4	3	2	1	
Out of humility, I ask						Out of arrogance, I demand
I am approachable by those in need						Those in need avoid me and are afraid to bother me
I allow the Lord to defend the authority He has given me						I grasp for authority and am self-defensive in holding on to it
I am willing to forgive my accusers						I want to "make them pay"
I am merciful to my enemies when they are defeated						I gloat over the fall of my enemies
I give of myself, laboring for the benefits of others						I act with my own interests in mind – "what's in it for me?!"
I am not easily provoked						I am quarrelsome
I am a biblical peace-maker						I am always "looking for a fight"
I pursue gentleness						I am the way I am . . . "take it or leave it!"
I am patient and endure long						I reach "my limit" quickly
When I correct others, I try to teach them the why and how of things						When I correct others, it is usually a matter of brute "because I said so!"
When I correct others, I give opportunity for them to repent						My "correction" throws the book at them and then slams the bars shut
I don't "talk bad" about people behind their backs						I often speak evil of others
I am courteous to all people						I am courteous to those I deem worthy
I am reasonable and prayerful in my responses						My anxious and turmoil-filled heart taints my responses to others
I am jealous only for the glory of God and ambitious for His kingdom						I am motivated by bitter jealousy and selfish ambition
I am meek						I am ruthless, scoffing at the powerless and using my words to ensnare them.
I am respectful of even those who strongly oppose the truth						I am willing to "slice and dice" those who persecute Christians
I treat my wife in an understanding way						My wife had better "understand" me, or else!
I discipline and instruct my children						I provoke my kids with arbitrary displays of "authority"
I am kind even to ungrateful and evil people						I love only those who love me
I seek to redemptively restore those caught in sin						I am judgmental and harsh, "throw the bums out!"
I REFLECT THE MEEKNESS AND GENTLENESS OF CHRIST						**I REFLECT THE BRUTAL GRASPING FOR AND USE OF POWER LIKE SATAN**

PRAYERS FOR RESTORING THE JUDGMENT OF CHARITY

During painful conflict, it is very difficult and perhaps impossible to restore the Judgment of Charity through an exercise of our wills. We desperately need Jesus and the Holy Spirit's empowerment. The following three simple prayers express our hearts as we come to the Savior. Perhaps they will help you as you come to Him.

The Prayer of Relinquishment:

Father, as I come to You, **the Righteous Judge,**
I relinquish my will.
I let go of my judgment of others' motives.
I give You my stony heart
and TRUST that in Your time, You will do what is right.

The Prayer of Suffering:

Lord, as I come to You, **my Strong Defender,**
I wait by Jesus in the Garden of Gethsemane,
remembering the weight of my sins.
I lower my defenses and open myself again
to TRUST amid the suffering that You allow.

The Prayer of Love:

Savior, as I come to You, **my Loving Redeemer,**
I ask for strength to do what is right.
Grant me what I need to
help make a way for reconciliation,
even when I do not feel like it.
Help me TRUST that You will restore my joy and peace.

MEDIATION TRIAGE – Three Session Instructions

SESSION ONE

a) **Pray** for the individuals and your time together with them.

b) **Ask them to share** what's happening in their relationship.
   i) Be certain to listen to both sides, which may take direct questions asked of one or both.
   ii) Help them clarify what are the top 2-3 issues that are hurting their relational satisfaction.

c) **Share with them the Cycle of Conflict.**
   i) Where possible, use illustrations of what they just shared to show where they are in the cycle.
   ii) In all likelihood they will be in either the "Injustice Gathering / You're Wrong" or perhaps the "Confrontation / Let's Fight" stage.
   iii) Help them understand that crossing the line from stage 2's "Role Dilemma / What's Wrong" to the third stage eventually involves losing the Judgment of Charity.
   iv) Define the Judgment of Charity if they have never heard of the concept before.
   v) Explain how the loss of the Judgment of Charity so impacts our filters that it is almost impossible to work on a relationship until it is restored (at least to some degree).

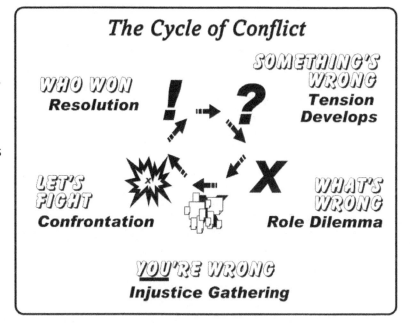

d) **Explain the two hands of forgiveness.**
   i) This gives you an opportunity to share the Gospel.
   ii) Explain why forgiveness is essential to any long-term relationships that involve sinful humans.

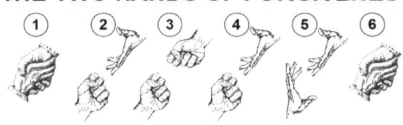

THE TWO HANDS OF FORGIVENESS

1. We were created to have fellowship with our Creator.

2. But we chose to sin and rebel against God (shaking our fist at Him).

3. And the Holy Perfect God was righteously angry with us for our rebellion. He closed His fist in judgment of our sin.

4. But God so loved us that He extended forgiveness (opening His hand) to the whole world through the work of His Son, Jesus. Yet that does not mean that the whole world is forgiven. God honors us by giving us a choice. We must respond in order to be forgiven.

5. We open our hand to receive God's gift by turning away from our sin in repentance and asking for forgiveness, trusting by faith in the work of Jesus.

6. Now the forgiveness is "complete" because we are reconciled to God in restored fellowship with Him as our Creator and Redeemer.

e) Share the "Sins and Resentments" exercise.

HIS LISTS

SINS	RESENTMENTS

HER LISTS

SINS	RESENTMENTS

i) **Explain how they are to prepare to make two lists,** with the headings "Sins" and "Resentments."

ii) **Review the commitment to wait alone on God for one undistracted hour.**

   (1) This time begins by each person asking the Holy Spirit to reveal to them any sins that they have committed against the other.

   (a) *These may be sins of commission or omission.*

   (b) *These sins are written on their "Sins" list.*

   (c) *These items must be specific. General statements like, "I've been unthoughtful" are not as helpful as, "I've was unthoughtful when I did not remember our anniversary."*

   (2) After the point where no additional sins are being brought to mind by the Holy Spirit, the person prays again. This time the request is for help in being honest about the resentments or bitterness they have toward the other person for sins they have committed against them.

   (a) *Again, these may be sins the other party has committed, or things left undone (sins of commission OR omission).*

   (b) *These are written on their "Resentments" list.*

iii) Go over how these lists will be used to help restore the Judgment of Charity.

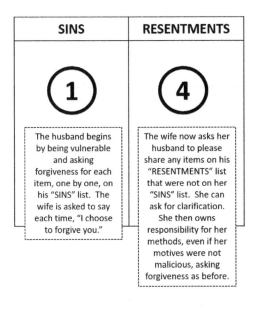

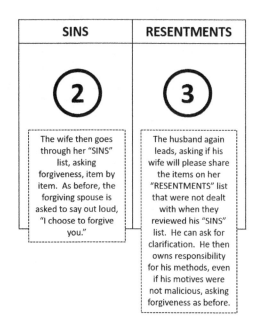

(1) We will review the first person's "Sins" list. In a marriage, we begin with the husband.
  (a) *The individual will be asked to confess their "SINS" list, one at time.*
  (b) *If the sins are vague, you will ask for a clarification or an example of when he was "unthoughtful" (or whatever general statement he made).*
  (c) *After confessing the sin, the husband is to look his wife in the eyes and ask, "Would you please forgive me for this?"*
  (d) *The wife then considers and (hopefully) chooses to offer forgiveness for the specific sin by stating, "I forgive you for . . . (restatement of the sin)."*

(2) Review the other person's "Sins" list (comparable to #1 above). In a marriage, this would be the wife's sin list.

(3) The first party then asks the other party to share the items on their "RESENTMENTS" list that did not get taken care of (crossed off) when they confessed their "SINS" list items.
  (a) More than likely, these remaining items were not "intended" by the first party, but they still have to understand them and own responsibility for them.
  (b) As the first party "owns" the items, even if they had good motives, they then ask for forgiveness for these "methods", one at a time.

(4) The other individual then asks the first party to share his "RESENTMENTS" list (as described in #3).

f) **Reassure the individuals** that this process is not a "quick fix" but rather a serious attempt at restoring the Judgment of Charity.
   i) Some people will sometimes want to do the confessing and forgiving without the mediator present. If this comes up, you will need to make a judgment call on whether this is a good idea or not.
      (1) Based on the limited severity of the problems and an apparent lower threshold of emotional pain, some folks may be allowed to go through the exercise alone and merely report back at the next session. This is the exception to the rule.
      (2) Much more commonly, you will ask that they share their confessions and offers of forgiveness in front of you for the following reasons:
         (a) You will be there praying quietly as they go through the steps, seeking the Spirit's help for them to be vulnerable and able to hear each other.
         (b) You can help make sure that the process does not get side-tracked by one volatile item.
         (c) You can help "translate" what one person may be saying, even when they aren't saying it well.
         (d) You can observe the process and begin to see some patterns of things that might need to change for there to be lasting health in the relationship.

g) **Set the next session's date, time, and place.**

h) **Pray together.**
   i) Holding hands may be appropriate.
   ii) Ask all parties to pray. If a couple, ask the man to go first.
      (1) If they are uncomfortable, give them a "sample prayer" that they could say. For example, "Lord, thanks that you are the God Who restores. Please restore our relationship and make it even better than before. Help us as we make our lists to listen to You."
   iii) Close the prayer time and session by leading in prayer (after their prayers).

SESSION TWO

a) **Pray for the individuals** and your time together with them.

b) **Review the "Sins and Resentments" Lists (using the order described earlier)**
   i) Have them face each other and speak to each other (not you).
   ii) As they go through the process, observe (and perhaps jot down) any observations you have about the following:
      (1) How they are going through the steps? Guardedly? Vulnerably? Flippantly?
      (2) How they are talking to each other? Respectful? Disdainful? Patronizing?
      (3) Are there patterns to the items on the lists, ways that they could be "grouped" together to fall under a heading?
   iii) Review the first person's "Sins" list. With a couple, this will be the man's list.
      (1) They will be asked to confess their "SINS" list, one at a time.
         (a) If the sins are vague, ask for a clarification or example of when they were "unthoughtful" (or whatever general statement they made).
         (b) After confessing the sin, the party making the confession is to look into the eyes of the other and ask, "Would you please forgive me for this?"
      (2) The other party will then consider and (hopefully) choose to offer forgiveness for the specific sin by stating, "I forgive you for . . . . . (restatement of the sin)."
   iv) Review the second party's "Sins" list (as described in #1 above). With a couple, this will be her list.
   v) The first party then asks the other to share the items on their "RESENTMENTS" list that did not get taken care of (crossed off) when they confessed their "SINS" list items.
      (1) More than likely, these remaining items were not "intended" but the first party still has to understand them and own responsibility for them.
      (2) As they own the items, even if they had good motives, they then asks for forgiveness for them one at a time.
   vi) The second party then asks the first to share their "RESENTMENTS" list (as described in #3).

c) **Rejoice** in their openness to the process of confession and forgiveness. **Affirm** them for going through the steps taken.

d) **Ask if they noticed any patterns** in their relationship being revealed by the confession and forgiveness process.
   i) Confirm any that they share that you noticed as well.
   ii) Present any additional patterns you noticed and ask them to discuss whether they agree or disagree with your observations.

TWO CUPS ILLUSTRATION OF RELATIONSHIPS
Gerhard T. deBock

- As singles, our cups have been filled to different levels.
- We also have leaks in our cups and "thin spots" that can easily be broken.
- When we come to Christ we can allow Him to fill our cups and heal our holes & thin spots.

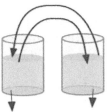

- In the early stages of a relationship we usually work hard at filling each other's cups, making certain that we don't tear through their thin spots.
- A strong "Judgment of Charity" tends to seal many of the small leaks.

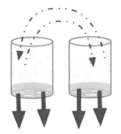

- Unresolved hurts and disappointments create holes, often tearing open the thin spots. The resulting loss of the Judgment of Charity means that even the good that is put into the cup just runs through.
- Those with low "love tanks" give less to others.

- It is critical that we stop the "sieve effect" by closing up the holes through confession and forgiveness. We must change the sieves back into cups, so that we can catch the acts of love that are given.

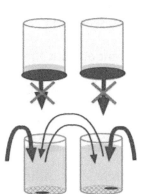

- Asking God to fill our cups is essential.
- Avoiding creating holes or tearing through the other person's thin spots is part of repentance.
- Actively choosing to serve the other by filling their cup with acts of love, according to their love language.

e) **Assign the following exercises.**
   i) **"Hole Makers"**
      (1) Ask them to write down what they each believe tend to be the two worst "hole makers" in their relationship.
         (a) These are actions tear holes in their "cups," causing the joy to run low in their walk with each other.
         (b) These may well be related to the patterns they noticed from the "Sins and Resentments" lists.
   ii) **"Cup Fillers"**
      (1) Ask them to write down what they believe could be 4 great ways that the other person could "fill their cups of love."
f) **Set the next session's date, time, and place.**
g) **Pray together.** (Use same pattern as session one)

SESSION THREE

a) **Pray for the individuals** and your time together with them.

b) **Have them share their "hole makers" and "cup fillers" with each other.**
   i) Review the "Hole Makers"
      (1) The first party, in a marriage it would be the husband, is encouraged to ask the other, "What do I tend to do that really tears a hole in your heart and robs joy from our relationship?"
         (a) The other party is directed to share, speaking the truth in love.
            (i) Specifically, they are taught to say, "Though you may not mean to, it hurts me when you . . ."
            (ii) This is applying the lesson of giving love regarding another's motives, while speaking truth about their methods (or the impact of those methods).
         (b) After they share, the first party (e.g. the husband) is encouraged to make a declaration that they will intentionally work on "putting off" those specific behaviors.
      (2) The second party is then encouraged to ask the same question about hole makers (similar process to above).
   ii) Review the "Cup Fillers"
      (1) The first party (husband) is encouraged to ask, "What 4 things could I do that would really help you feel like I value, respect and love you?"
         (a) After they share, the first party is then to ask, "Which of these are the top two?"
      (2) The second party (wife) is then instructed to follow the same pattern.

c) **Review with them what is their understanding of the top "hole makers" and "cup fillers."**
   i) Encourage them to write these down and to review them daily for at least three weeks, making them a matter of prayer and action.

d) **Discuss with them what additional steps** might help their relationship to continue to grow and rebuilt trust.
   i) Refer to professional, longer term counseling if needed.
   ii) If married, consider suggesting that they go through Marital Mentoring with another couple.
   iii) Perhaps they will want to schedule a follow-up phone call with you in two months to see how they are doing. This would help them to know that you are committed to expecting accountability.

e) **Pray together.**
   i) Use the same pattern as session one.

MEDIATOR TRIAGE WORKSHEETS

MEDIATOR TRIAGE WORKSHEET - SESSION ONE:

- ☐ PRAYER
- ☐ ASK THEM TO SHARE WHAT'S HAPPENING IN THEIR RELATIONSHIP (take notes and listen actively)
- ☐ SHARE CYCLE OF CONFLICT AS TIED TO THEIR EXAMPLES

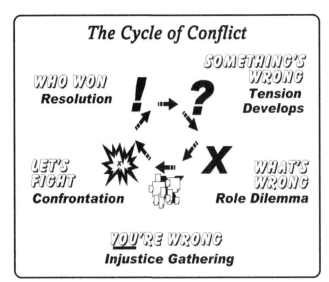

NOTE WHEN THE JUDGMENT OF CHARITY TENDS TO BE LOST (between the second and third stages)

NOTE THAT THE CYCLE EASILY DEGENERATES INTO THE DEATH SPIRAL

- ☐ EXPLAIN THE TWO HANDS OF FORGIVENESS

THE TWO HANDS OF FORGIVENESS

1. We were created to have fellowship with our Creator.

2. But we chose to sin and rebel against God (shaking our fist at Him).

3. And the Holy Perfect God was righteously angry with us for our rebellion. He closed His fist in judgment of our sin.

4. But God so loved us that He extended forgiveness (opening His hand) to the whole world through the work of His Son, Jesus. Yet that does not mean that the whole world is forgiven. God honors us by giving us a choice. We must respond in order to be forgiven.

5. We open our hand to receive God's gift by turning away from our sin in repentance and asking for forgiveness, trusting by faith in the work of Jesus.

6. Now the forgiveness is "complete" because we are reconciled to God in restored fellowship with Him as our Creator and Redeemer.

☐ SHARE THE "SINS AND RESENTMENTS" LISTS EXERCISE

SINS	RESENTMENTS

SINS	RESENTMENTS

☐ REVIEW HOW THE LISTS WILL BE REVIEWED

SINS	RESENTMENTS
1	**4**
The husband begins by being vulnerable and asking forgiveness for each item, one by one, on his "SINS" list. The wife is asked to say each time, "I choose to forgive you."	The wife now asks her husband to please share any items on his "RESENTMENTS" list that were not on her "SINS" list. She can ask for clarification. She then owns responsibility for her methods, even if her motives were not malicious, asking forgiveness as before.

SINS	RESENTMENTS
2	**3**
The wife then goes through her "SINS" list, asking forgiveness, item by item. As before, the forgiving spouse is asked to say out loud, "I choose to forgive you."	The husband again leads, asking if his wife will please share the items on her "RESENTMENTS" list that were not dealt with when they reviewed his "SINS" list. He can ask for clarification. He then owns responsibility for his methods, even if his motives were not malicious, asking forgiveness as before.

☐ REASSURE THAT THIS IS NOT A QUICK FIX BUT AN EFFORT TO RESTORE THE JUDGMENT OF CHARITY

☐ SET NEXT SESSION'S DATE, TIME, PLACE

☐ PRAYER TOGETHER (Everyone prays)

THE
JUDGMENT OF CHARITY

I CHOOSE TO GIVE YOU THE JUDGMENT OF CHARITY BY MAKING THE ACTIVE CHOICE TO SEEK A VERDICT REGARDING YOUR MOTIVES IN THE COURT OF GOD'S

LOVE

This means that I choose to
Entrust ultimate judgment to God.
while
Lowering my self-centered defenses
and
Making a way by assuming the best motives possible

138

MEDIATOR TRIAGE WORKSHEET - SESSION TWO:

☐ PRAYER
☐ REVIEW SINS AND RESENTMENTS LISTS

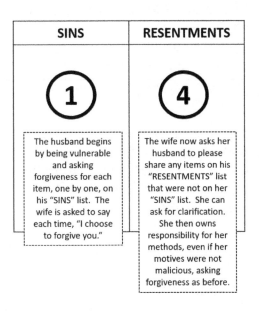
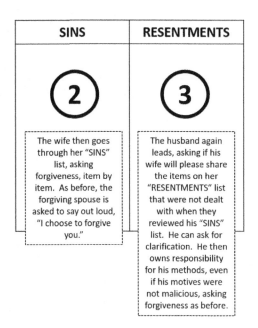

☐ REJOICE IN THEIR OPENNESS. AFFIRM THEM FOR THEIR COURAGE.

☐ ASK IF THEY NOTICED ANY PATTERNS IN WHAT THEY SHARED

☐ ASSIGN THE HOLE MAKERS AND CUP FILLERS EXERCISE (see next page)

☐ SET NEXT SESSION'S DATE, TIME, PLACE

☐ PRAYER TOGETHER (Everyone prays)

TWO CUPS ILLUSTRATION OF RELATIONSHIPS

Gerhard T. deBock

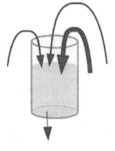

- As singles, our cups have been filled to different levels.
- We also have leaks in our cups and "thin spots" that can easily be broken.
- When we come to Christ we can allow Him to fill our cups and heal our holes & thin spots.

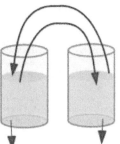

- In the early stages of a relationship we usually work hard at filling each other's cups, making certain that we don't tear through their thin spots.
- A strong "Judgment of Charity" tends to seal many of the small leaks.

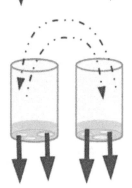

- Unresolved hurts and disappointments create holes, often tearing open the thin spots. The resulting loss of the Judgment of Charity means that even the good that is put into the cup just runs through.
- Those with low "love tanks" give less to others.

- It is critical that we stop the "sieve effect" by closing up the holes through confession and forgiveness. We must change the sieves back into cups, so that we can catch the acts of love that are given.

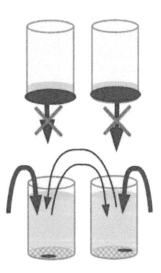

- Asking God to fill our cups is essential.
- Avoiding creating holes or tearing through the other person's thin spots is part of repentance.
- Actively choosing to serve the other by filling their cup with acts of love, according to their love language.

140

MEDIATOR TRIAGE WORKSHEET - SESSION THREE:

☐ PRAYER

☐ HAVE THEM SHARE THEIR HOLE MAKERS AND CUP FILLERS LISTS WITH EACH OTHER

Use the following questions as a guide. They are written with a marriage situation in mind.

- *(Both, husband first) "What do I tend to do that really tears a hole in your heart and robs joy from our marriage?"*

- *(Both, in response to the question above) "Though you may not mean to, it hurts me when you (do this OR don't to this)"*

- *(Husband) "What 4 things could I do that would really help you feel cherished and secure?" "Which of these are the top two?"*

- *(Wife) "What 4 things could I do that would help you feel honored and respected?" "Which of these are the top two?"*

☐ HAVE INDIVIDUALS WRITE UP A COVENANT OF ACTION STEPS FOR THE NEXT 3-6 WEEKS.

This will be based on avoiding the hole makers and pursuing the cup fillers.

Often this is done after the third session.

If married, encourage the husband to take the lead.

Create accountability by having them send it to you, perhaps by email.

Assure them that you will use the covenant as a basis to pray for them consistently.

☐ CREATE A TRACK POINT THAT GIVES A POINT OF ACCOUNTABILITY FOR THEM IN THE NEAR FUTURE.

This is important to help ensure new patterns of relating to each other.

You may refer to professional counseling or marital mentoring.

☐ PRAYER TOGETHER (Everyone prays)

CASE STUDIES

The following case studies are designed to help you see whether you can apply the concepts and commitments of a peacemaker.

The workshop training, that this material was originally designed for, encourages the participants to bring in several of their own case studies. The names and identifying details are removed or changed. The individuals are given some time to consider their thoughts on how to pursue peace. Then the group works on the case together.

"I appeal to you, brothers, by the name of our Lord Jesus Christ, that all of you agree, and that there be no divisions among you, but that you be united in the same mind and the same judgment."

1 Corinthians 1:10

INSTRUCTIONS

1. **Review the case study.**

2. **Jot down notes on how you believe you should/could respond, as a biblical peacemaker.**

   Do this before looking at Gary's thoughts.

3. **Review Gary's thoughts.**

   *These will **assess the assumptions,** including the folks' in the case study and ours. He will also present some **clarifying questions** that may help bring insight to the situation. Finally, **biblical concepts** that bring hope and truth will be covered. These will help us be encouragers to those ensnared in conflict.*

   In this section, reference will be made to definitions and discussions in the reference tool, "Fighting for the Judgment of Charity." Items in ALL CAPITALS can be found in the glossary at the end of this workbook.

4. **Prayerfully consider actual conflict situations.**

   Think through past or present conflict situations that you are aware of, to which you could apply some of the insights you have gained. Capture these thoughts.

   Follow through on what God is asking you to do.

CASE STUDY 1

"I've got the facts. We're talking about the facts, what really happened. We are not going to let this go because of a weasel figuring a way to slink out of trouble. Especially based on some 'technicality.'"

The anger in their voice is matched by the harshness of their facial expression. As a mediator, should you reprimand this person because they have lost the judgment of charity? Do we know for certain that they have lost the judgment of love? Or, are we rendering a decision about their motives based on our interpretation of their methods? If we confront them, are we about to do what we want to accuse them of?

My Thoughts on how I could/should respond

<u>Gary's Thoughts</u>

Most of us would assume that this person assumes that they have no FILTERS and therefore they have no bias in looking at the "facts." We might *"assume that they assume"* that the other person is the problem, they are a guilty weasel who wants to avoid accountability. It would be difficult for us not to assume that they have lost the JUDGMENT OF CHARITY.

Instead of confronting them with our judgment about their MOTIVES, it would probably be more helpful to ask them about their METHODS. We could ask permission to mirror back to them what we heard them say and how they said it. This would be the process of our "CHECKING IT OUT." We graciously seek to either confirm or correct our assumptions.

We could ask them if they've ever heard of the CYCLE OF CONFLICT. Reviewing it with them, we can point to the place where the focus changes from WHAT'S WRONG to YOU'RE WRONG. This is where the JUDGMENT OF CHARITY is usually lost. While expressing empathy for the pain they have been through, we can also help them to see that the pattern of their on-going conflict is quite common, and therefore there is hope.

We must be careful not to imagine that we can MIND-READ, nor should we PIGEON-HOLE the other person. It is difficult for us not to prejudge the situation because of the FILTERS of our past experiences, whether our own conflicts or those we have helped mediate.

<u>Prayerful Reflection</u>

Ask God to bring to your mind conflicts you have been in or know about. What insights from this case study could be applied? Additionally, are there concepts and strategies that you did not originally consider, but now realize you need to incorporate into your thinking?

CASE STUDY 2

She just got done responding with tears. Then, with a stern voice, she starts to give an answer to your question about what's happened to her relationship. The words seem harsh and cutting.

In the other chair, with pursed lips, he is struggling to make or, at least, keep eye contact with anyone. After a few moments of awkward silence, you ask him, "Do you agree? Is that the heart of the problem?" Measured words respond, "Well, yes, but . . ." His response moves from defending his intentions to blaming her for making him act in ways he really doesn't want to.

She retorts, first by squirming in her seat, then sitting up straighter, shaking her head in disagreement. Finally, she blurts out, "No way! You're not going to put all that on me. If I'm that way at all, it is because of the way you've treated me."

As a mediator, how can you bring hope to such deep pain, resentment and blaming?

My Thoughts on how I could/should respond

Gary's Thoughts

On-going, unresolved conflict is usually riddled with pain. The wounds, whether deep or shallow, are usually infected with some strain of bitterness. One of the key indicators that the JUDGMENT OF CHARITY has been lost is the presence of blaming. This is especially true when we blame others for our actions or attitudes. At times, this blaming will present itself in the form of defensiveness, guarding ourselves by justifying our actions as a retaliation for theirs.

It is very appropriate to ask permission to pray for the situation and those involved. Doing so models the concept of a TIME OUT. Inviting God's Spirit to give wisdom and insight brings the hope of the involvement of the Wonderful Counselor.

The mediator will often be asked to take sides or to act as a judge of who is right and wrong. Rarely will such a posture bring lasting peace to the relationship. More helpful is to actively listen and then suggest that we may see a pattern in what they are experiencing. After asking if we can share what we see, we can review their situation while presenting the stages of the cycle of conflict.

Note the point in the cycle where the JUDGMENT OF CHARITY is lost. Ask what the difference is between the WHAT'S WRONG and the YOU'RE WRONG stages. Encourage some reflection on what their apparent blaming of each other indicates about what stage their conflict is in.

If the conflict has been long-standing, share the DEATH SPIRAL pattern. Note how repeated wounds make it very hard NOT to go right back to INJUSTICE GATHERING, even over little things. Ask them to compare their situation to these patterns.

Share why it is important to take responsibility for our own actions. Another person's bad behavior does not justify ours. God's grace can break through even deeply infected conflict when we humble ourselves and ask that He change us first. God gives grace to the humble.

Prayerful Reflection

Ask God to bring to your mind conflicts you have been in or know about. What insights from this case study could be applied? Additionally, are there concepts and strategies that you did not originally consider, but now realize you need to incorporate into your thinking?

CASE STUDY 3

"That's just how they are. Nothing's going to change them. How am I supposed to honor my father and mother when they always seem to know how to crush my spirit by being judgmental and demeaning? It is easier just to avoid them altogether."

As a mediator, you seek a bit more clarification, asking them whether their parents claim to be followers of Jesus. Answering quickly, she says, "Oh, sure. They wouldn't miss church for anything. Dad has even served as a deacon."

Should we, as peacemakers, give counsel to these professing believers? Or should we just agree with their assessment? Should we absolve them of any further responsibility to do something more? What would be some wise biblical counsel?

My Thoughts on how I could/should respond

Gary's Thoughts

It is very difficult for a friendly conversation to NOT drift into GOSSIP when we are talking negatively about others. The conflict in this case study, between adult children and their parents, is not one in which we are directly involved (we are not the parents nor the children). If we do not try to redeem the conversation, the three warning sirens of GOSSIP will all go off. The parents are not present (behind their backs) and they are saying hard things (talking "bad"). If we don't redirect, the third siren will sound because the folks will be merely venting, which is not for the good purpose of seeking reconciliation.

After expressing EMPATHY, it may be appropriate to ask if we can help these friends think through how they might try and find a biblical path toward true peace in this relationship. If they are not willing to do that, we must express clearly your discomfort and unwillingness to "talk bad behind people's backs."

If they seem open to "peace-making," then we can explore their assumptions. It seems that this person is assuming that "you can't teach an old dog new tricks." They have little hope that anything will change in the relationship and that, perhaps, it is better to just avoid the parents rather than have another blow-up or melt-down. They also may not realize that their withdrawal has meant that the parents have needed to "guess" what their motives are for these evasive methods. These are things that should be explored further.

It will also be important to clarify if they have followed up with the biblical teaching on ESCALATING CARE-FRONTING, per MATTHEW 18's teaching. If they have not, we should review the steps with them and then ask if we can help them prayerfully work through what the next right thing to do is.

Prayerful Reflection

Ask God to bring to your mind conflicts you have been in or know about. What insights from this case study could be applied? Additionally, are there concepts and strategies that you did not originally consider, but now realize you need to incorporate into your thinking?

CASE STUDY 4

"I left because of his arrogance and the awful decisions he made. I wasn't going to submit myself or my family to that kind of leadership. That's not how leaders are supposed to act."

You seek to point toward reconciliation and peace by asking, "Did you talk with him before you left?"

"We tried. He just defended himself and his actions. I don't think he even really listened to us. So, we just left."

As a peacemaker, how can you turn this venting, and possibly even a bout of gossip, into something productive?

My Thoughts on how I could/should respond

151

Gary's Thoughts

We don't know the context of this conversation, but it seems to include some VENTING of hurt feelings. If it is not turned toward reconciliation, the talking about this leader's perceived arrogance certainly is saying bad things behind his back.

There are many questions that should be explored, if the individual is open to seeking what God would want. Perhaps, this is the place to ask, "Do you believe you have done what God wants of you? Are there things you wish you had done differently?"

Additional clarification may come by asking, "How would you know if this leader did listen to you?" And, "Did he try to make contact after you left? If so, how? What was your response?"

A vital point of clarification would be, "You expressed very strong criticism of his arrogance and un-teachable-ness, let alone his awful decisions. Do you believe that this leader sinned in his actions?"

If we assume both of the parties are professing Christ-followers, then this last inquiry begins to make clear the next right thing to do. If this individual saw his brother sinning, especially against himself, then he is mandated by MATTHEW 18 and other passages to care-front and escalate, if needed. From what we've read, there has been only one attempt and no ESCALATION after that failed.

If the individual says there was no sin, just a disagreement on priorities or something similar, then we take a different approach. Gently we could ask, "Do you believe that the way you left was God-honoring?" "How serious do you think division is within the body of Christ?

Either way, the wound seems infected. We should ask them whether they are open to our joining them in a prayer, seeking a way forward toward reconciliation?

Prayerful Reflection

Ask God to bring to your mind conflicts you have been in or know about. What insights from this case study could be applied? Additionally, are there concepts and strategies that you did not originally consider, but now realize you need to incorporate into your thinking?

CASE STUDY 5

"I wrote a long email to him, outlining my concerns about the direction of the ministry. All he wrote back was that he would rather talk about this face to face. Well, I really don't feel comfortable doing that. I'd rather think about my responses carefully and wordsmith them wisely. His unwillingness to talk my language means that he really doesn't care about me or my concerns. So, I left the ministry. But, my hands are clean because I, at least, tried. Jesus doesn't ask any more than that of me."

Should you agree with this person, that their hands are "clean" in this conflict situation? What are the ramifications of saying nothing about this ongoing division?

My Thoughts on how I could/should respond

Gary's Thoughts

Perceived assumptions that need to be explored include whether they believe that the other party's unwillingness to write long emails means that they don't care about the relationship? Also, whether "clean hands" before God only requires that we try once, and that in our own preferred way. And, that there is no need to escalate nor to bring in others to help.

Questions I would ask, even if I were this person's spouse, include, "Do you consider their decisions sinful? How so?" "Did you try to escalate the conflict, seeking the help of a mediator or in bringing someone with you as a witness of the conflict per MATTHEW 18?" "Do you believe your current posture, including what you tell others about this situation, is truly 'pursuing peace?'"

So many conflicts between professing believers are about matters that are "wise-unwise" rather than "not sinful-sinful." Unfortunately, we easily allow ourselves off the hook in needing to escalate care-fronting, because it is not a "sin" issue. Yet, the level of hurt and bitterness, even animus and resulting division, makes it seem like someone is treating another "like a tax-gatherer or Gentile."

Prayerful Reflection

Ask God to bring to your mind conflicts you have been in or know about. What insights from this case study could be applied? Additionally, are there concepts and strategies that you did not originally consider, but now realize you need to incorporate into your thinking?

CASE STUDY 6

"It is my decision, if I stay or leave this church. I became a member because I agreed with the doctrines and directions of this local body. But, the board's decisions have made it clear that they have changed course. So, I am out of here! If they want to know why, they can find me and ask. Even if they do, and I doubt they will, I am never going back."

As a friend, who noticed this person's absence and then received this reply to your inquiry about what's going on, what should your next move be?

My Thoughts on how I could/should respond

Gary's Thoughts

The pain and hurt of conflict can prod even professing Christians into saying things more absolutely and vehemently than they really intend. If this individual were asked, "Do you mean that if they called you, spoke openly with you, and listened to your concerns, that you still wouldn't even consider going back?" They perhaps would soften their rhetoric. A follow-up question might be, "What if they admitted their error and were willing to make it right?"

Asking such hypotheticals can help us explore, along with the other person, what is going on in their hearts. Their FILTERS may be clogged with past experiences involving leaders who would not listen. While we may EMPATHIZE with their hurt, we should not allow them to be deceived into thinking that they have acted biblically.

If they are teachable, other questions may include, "Do you consider it the board's responsibility to know what you are thinking and to track you down so that they can hear you put those thoughts into words?" "Certainly, a wise board will initiate exit interview, but is it sinful not to do so?"

"Do you think it was rude of you to just leave?" "How do you think your decision, and how you carried it out, has impacted the testimony of the Gospel in your area?" "What have you told others when they have asked you why you've left the church?"

An important question may be, "Do you wish it could have ended better, even if you still had to leave? How do you imagine a "better" way would have looked?"

Prayerful Reflection

Ask God to bring to your mind conflicts you have been in or know about. What insights from this case study could be applied? Additionally, are there concepts and strategies that you did not originally consider, but now realize you need to incorporate into your thinking?

CASE STUDY 7

"He owes me an apology. Sure, we talked for hours. We even prayed together at the end of the second time we talked. But, he wasn't going to budge. He said that it was his call, a judgment call, he made after much prayer. So, we decided to distance ourselves from him. And, no, I'm not sure we made clear to him what the sin was that we think he was guilty of . . . but, we've been really hurt. His decision hurt our friend, and when you hurt our friend, you hurt us. To not break fellowship would be betraying our hurt friend, wouldn't it?"

You've stumbled into a conflict. You were merely saying, "Hi," as you passed each other in the grocery store. The carts you were pushing slowed a bit and you followed up with, "Hey, I haven't seen you at church for a while. Is everything OK?" In your mind, you were considering that perhaps they had been sick or traveling. But, when you got the answer above, you knew they were really "sick and tired" because of conflict. What do you do now?

<u>Gary's Thoughts</u>

The grocery aisle is not the right place to have a full-out discussion about so serious a matter. To <u>just</u> express EMPATHY, and even sorrow about their departure, may well come across as condoning their behavior. That includes their behavior in how they left a relationship AND how they are talking about it now.

Better would be a sincere offer to help seek a way to PURSUE PEACE. Ask them, "Would you be willing to meet with me to prayerfully consider how to resolve this conflict?"

If they are not willing, we must remind them that their request for an apology clearly suggests that they consider the other person to have sinned against them. Following the protocol found in MATTHEW 18 is not optional for Christ-followers. To not ESCALATE is sin. To leave without ESCALATING would leave less mature believers within the church vulnerable to abuse by this leader (if he is sinning).

If they are willing, we can set a time to meet or for us to call them. When we meet with them, we should probe the unwise or sinful things done (or left undone) that have lead to this break in fellowship. We can offer to be or to find a mediator who can go with them in escalating the care-fronting. While it is great that they talked and prayed with the individual several times, the result makes it clear that this is not a "CLEAN WOUND."

<u>Prayerful Reflection</u>

Ask God to bring to your mind conflicts you have been in or know about. What insights from this case study could be applied? Additionally, are there concepts and strategies that you did not originally consider, but now realize you need to incorporate into your thinking?

CASE STUDY 8

"He'll never change." That's what she said. The same refrain followed your reminder, that we should always have hope because God can change anyone. When you asked if we could try one more time, the refrain changed words, but the meaning was the same, "It won't do any good. He may say he's changed or that he wants to change. He may even say he has now trusted Jesus as Lord and Savior, but it is all just a show. He'll never change."

As a mediator, how can you help a person, who has lost hope, be more willing to biblically escalate the "care-fronting" of the sinful behaviors? They say they have tried again and again. Even the adult children have confronted him. "It won't matter if you or the church confronts him." Is there a danger to pushing such a person into trying one more time when they really have no hope that it will make any difference?

My Thoughts on how I could/should respond

Gary's Thoughts

The core question is whether we have responsibility to take initiative and try <u>even</u> when we don't believe it will do any good. While this individual has confronted again and again, the only ESCALATION has been through the voices of the kids, now adults.

Perhaps we've spoken with this man. He wants his marriage to work. He's even responded by trusting Jesus as Lord and Savior. He admits he has been a jerk. But, he has not been unfaithful to the marriage bed. And now, as a believer, he has no intention of deserting his wife.

At this point, we should comfort this lady. We may EMPATHIZE with her frustrations. But, her accumulated pain does not give her biblical grounds for divorce. Perhaps we could ask, "What could your husband do to help you begin to believe that he really has changed?"

Encourage her to ask for something that is very "strong," something that could convince her that he has truly REPENTED. Then take that to her husband. See if he is willing to manifest this specific FRUIT OF REPENTANCE. If he is willing, and she will not work on some steps toward reconciliation, she will need to be care-fronted per Matthew 18 steps.

We must make it clear that our judgment of whether a person will or will not change is NOT the final deciding factor for whether we do the right, biblical next step.

Prayerful Reflection

Ask God to bring to your mind conflicts you have been in or know about. What insights from this case study could be applied? Additionally, are there concepts and strategies that you did not originally consider, but now realize you need to incorporate into your thinking?

CASE STUDY 9

"Nothing seems to really change. He says he's sorry, but then he continues to be self-absorbed and self-centered in how he acts. I don't think he really loves me, because if he did, he would be a lot more thoughtful and kind. I'm tired of this crazy cycle of me putting up with it all, finally exploding, he apologizes, and maybe buys me a gift, and then we do it again. Nothing really ever changes. I'm sick of it. I deserve better than this!"

Over coffee, your conversation changes focus, away from the kids and to her marriage. You weren't really looking for such a deep conversation. But, how can you be a real friend and say nothing. Just nodding your head doesn't seem right. What could you say?

My Thoughts on how I could/should respond

Gary's Thoughts

"I agree that the cycle you are in sounds horrible. I'm sure you want things to change. What have you already tried to do to make things better?"

After listening to their answer, I would want to make sure that we turn the conversation away from GOSSIP and towards reconciliation and peace. One way to do this is to ask permission to share some insights about the typical CYCLE and STYLES of conflict.

Drawing out the CYCLE and then adding the DEATH SPIRAL can help you show EMPATHY, if we tie the instruction back to their specific situation. After explaining the judgment of charity and where it fits in the cycle, we might ask, "What have you just told me that might point to when you started to struggle to keep the judgment of charity? As I ask this, I'm not saying he isn't responsible for his METHODS. Rather, we want to make sure your judgment about his heart and MOTIVES is leaning toward being rooted in bitterness and hurt, rather than in love."

Depending on the direction of the conversation, it may also be helpful to talk about the STYLES. After introducing them, we can ask, "Which styles do you think you were using during the "putting up" stage? How about the "exploding" stage? Remind her that she has the greatest control over her own behaviors. We may have her consider, "What do you think would happen if you didn't act like a TEDDY BEAR until the SHARK explodes?" "What would change if you could learn to speak the TRUTH IN LOVE?"

We should share that there is a way to restore the JUDGMENT OF CHARITY, but it is difficult, though do-able. "Would you like me to share this path with you?" If her reply indicates she only wants to VENT, we must make it clear that we are uncomfortable talking bad behind someone's back without the purpose of moving toward reconciliation and peace.

If she is open, we can then introduce her to the power of the SINS & RESENTMENTS LISTS. This can be followed up by asking if she thinks going through this would be a good idea. If so, we continue by asking, "What will be the best way to present this tool to your husband for his consideration?"

If she is open but skeptical, still wondering if anything will really change, be patient. After all, her husband has apologized a lot in the past, but things haven't gotten better. We must reassure her that what we are suggesting is an ESCALATION of the conflict's urgency. The process will also help create ACCOUNTABILITY for specific changes in both his and her methods. We will be looking for more than just verbal statements of REPENTANCE. We will expect tangible FRUITS OF REPENTANCE.

If she is unwilling to do anything positive, as a friend and sister-in-Christ, we should consider CARE-FRONTING her. Perhaps, "I've introduced you to some tools that have helped a lot of people. If you don't think that I can help you, would you allow me to help you find someone you would trust to equip and lead you to do what God wants you to do to have a better marriage?"

CASE STUDY 10

You asked, "Have you forgiven them?" The response was, "Sure. I know that I'm supposed to forgive someone since I've been forgiven as a Christian. I have no bitterness or resentment. But, I know one thing for certain, I will never go to the same church with them again. I couldn't worship God knowing that they are in the same room."

How would you respond?

My Thoughts on how I could/should respond

163

Gary's Thoughts

Consider beginning with, "May I ask you some questions so that I can understand things a bit better?" If the answer is positive, probe their understanding of forgiveness. After listening carefully, we may want to ask if we can present how we understand biblical forgiveness. Using the TWO HANDS OF FORGIVENESS illustration would be very appropriate.

After the basic definitions are cleared up, mentioned that Romans 5 gives us a picture of how God's forgiveness leaves us rejoicing. We exult in the fact that we are now at peace with God, and more importantly, He is at peace with us. We rejoice in the ability to trust God, giving Him the JUDGMENT OF CHARITY, even when the METHODS of the suffering we are facing could make us doubt His MOTIVES. Real forgiveness rejoices at the thought of Jesus' return in glory and power as the Judge of all. After a brief review of this, ask, "Does your relationship currently, with these folks who have hurt you and whom you've said you've forgiven, reflect this kind of rejoicing? Is the way that you have forgiven them the same way God has forgiven you?"

The response to such biblical instruction may be defensiveness, which questions why we are being so judgmental. If this happens, remind them that we are merely looking at their METHODS, specifically of not being able to go to church together nor to even worship in the same room. "These strong reactions may be appropriate for those who have been church-disciplined and declared to be unbelievers. But, they do not fit with those you say you have forgiven."

This may lead to an expression of confusion about the nature of OFFERED, RECEIVED, AND COMPLETED FORGIVENESS. When these distinctions are not made clear, there often is a cheapening of forgiveness to be merely an internal emotional release.

Prayerful Reflection

Ask God to bring to your mind conflicts you have been in or know about. What insights from this case study could be applied? Additionally, are their there now realize you need to incorporate into your thinking?

CASE STUDY 11

"That's the third strike. I know they said they didn't even know what the first two whiffs were all about, but they still are 'out!' If they had any sensitivity or thoughtfulness, they would know what happened in my heart and how they've hurt me. They should realize that I've walked away from the pitcher's mound. They're out and I'm done."

Should we confront or comfort this person? Or a combination of the two? How?

My Thoughts on how I could/should respond

Gary's Thoughts

Perhaps we could begin by saying something like, "It seems obvious that you've been deeply hurt, and not just once. I don't want to minimize your pain, but how do you reconcile Jesus' teachings about forgiving 70 times 7 with your statement, 'Three strikes and you're out'? As a follower of Jesus, are you PURSUING PEACE in this relationship or just the absence of conflict by distancing yourself? If you are not PURSUING PEACE, why not? If so, is there some way that I can help?

Assumptions to explore include, "Does the other party's inability to know what the first two strikes were, or to grasp what has bothered you, automatically mean that they are insensitive?"

"How have you communicated with them about what's happened in your heart and the hurt that you have felt? How did they respond to your efforts to communicate?"

It may be helpful to ask permission to review the STYLES of conflict. Then ask, "Which styles do you think you used at different points in your relationship with the other party?"

As we do this, we may want to remind them that they have responsibility for their part in the conflict. This may include not speaking the TRUTH IN LOVE. And, choosing not to ESCALATE the conflict biblically and intentionally. Rather, they seemed to expect the other party to be able to MIND-READ.

Even if they say that they still love the other party, their definition of love is certainly weaker than 1 Corinthians 13 love. There we read that love does not add up a record of wrongs.

Prayerful Reflection

Ask God to bring to your mind conflicts you have been in or know about. What insights from this case study could be applied? Additionally, are there concepts and strategies that you did not originally consider, but now realize you need to incorporate into your thinking?

CASE STUDY 12

"You know he has already stepped out on me once before. I forgave him then. But now, he's gone and done it again. How can I forgive him again!? How can I ever trust him, even if I still love him? If I let him back into my life, my heart, and my bed, am I just being a gullible fool? Shouldn't I make him pay for what he's done? How else will he learn?!"

As a trusted mentor, how would you counsel your sister in Christ, who has been cheated on . . . again!?

My Thoughts on how I could/should respond

Gary's Thoughts

CHECK IT OUT and make sure that "stepping out" means having a sexual affair, breaking the one-flesh relationship. If it does, then this woman has biblical ground for a divorce. However, she is not obligated to seek a divorce.

The fear that seems to be expressed is that her forgiveness will be an expression of gullibility. If the forgiveness is not "deserved," then she will be acting like a patsy. If this is along the lines of what she is thinking, we should review the unmerited favor (grace) of God that leads to our forgiveness. This helps us see that forgiveness cannot be earned. It is a gift, not a wage.

How then do we not get taken by someone who is posing as a penitent, but is not really planning on changing their ways? This is really a challenging heart issue. Peter certainly struggled with it when Jesus said we are to forgive 70 times 7. Luke 17 tells us to forgive every time they say they repent. This woman seems scared of being burned again, and rightly so. How can we help?

Critical is helping her understand the difference between REPENTANCE and the FRUITS OF REPENTANCE. Only God can look into a person's heart and know whether their statement of REPENTANCE is real. The rest of us must wait to see the tangible FRUITS OF REPENTANCE of changed METHODS.

This doesn't mean that we don't EXTEND FORGIVENESS until we see the FRUITS OF REPENTANCE. Rather, we understand that the process of healing toward complete restoration takes time. Trust has to be rebuilt.

If we don't EXTEND FORGIVENESS, then we will not be able to restore a measure of the JUDGMENT OF CHARITY. Without that we will never be able to "see" the FRUITS OF REPENTANCE as genuine. Without the JUDGMENT OF CHARITY, we will easily fall into the assumption that every "stumble" on their part is evidence that they really haven't repented. This could be true even if they have taken 15 healthy steps before the one stumble. This judgmental demand for perfection is one that we certainly don't expect of ourselves.

Prayerful Reflection

Ask God to bring to your mind conflicts you have been in or know about. What insights from this case study could be applied? Additionally, are there concepts and strategies that you did not originally consider, but now realize you need to incorporate into your thinking?

CASE STUDY 13

"I'm the good one in this marriage. I've borne up with his tirades and demands. I'm the one who always gives in. he always gets his way. Oh, yes, he thinks he's a great leader. But, when I think of the damage he has done to me, let alone to the kids, I can't let this go on. Won't you please go and talk to him? I think he'll listen to you."

How should you respond?

Gary's Thoughts

It hurts to hear someone in pain. We may be tempted to try to "rescue" them by becoming a conflict "hit man." For those who PURSUE PEACE, we can't contract out our CARE-FRONTING. If we really want to help, we must equip others to take responsibility and action themselves. For us to act on what we've just heard her say would be acting on HEARSAY.

To do nothing would be unkind. So, we should offer to help her ESCALATE the conflict and go with her to talk with her husband. We need her to go with us since she is the eye-witness of the sin. She may, perhaps, give us permission to call the husband and set up a time to all meet, but not for the actual CARE-FRONTING. We have not been direct witnesses of anything that she has accused him of.

Often the challenge is helping this self-proclaimed TEDDY BEAR or TURTLE take the responsibility for not ESCALATING the care-fronting with her sinning husband when the behavior continued. Gently, we must help her see that VENTING to her girl-friends or kids, but doing nothing, is gossip.

We can assure this sister that we won't let the confrontation get out of hand. It is our job to be the referee. If she is fearful for her safety, then we must be ready to help her get out temporarily. The CARE-FRONTING can then be done in a neutral place. The separation would continue until she feels it is safe to go home.

It may help to know why this woman is so hesitant. It may be tied to a fear of retaliation when there is no mediator present. Or, to the shame of "doing our dirty laundry in public."

It is critical to help her see that inaction hurts her, the kids, the testimony of the Gospel, and her husband. She must love all of them enough to bravely deal with the issue. It is a very hard thing to do, but to not do it may well may her complicit in her husband's sins.

Prayerful Reflection

Ask God to bring to your mind conflicts you have been in or know about. What insights from this case study could be applied? Additionally, are there concepts and strategies that you did not originally consider, but now realize you need to incorporate into your thinking?

CASE STUDY 14

"Who are you to judge me? Whether I get a divorce or not is my decision. And, I've decided that I've had enough. She may claim to be a Christ-follower, but she sure doesn't act like it. I've given her lots of chances. She just doesn't make me feel loved anymore. Why didn't the elders of the church get involved before now? Now, when it is all over isn't the time to stick your noses in. I'm leaving this stupid church."

As an elder who just found out about the impending divorce, you've gotten this response when you initiated a conversation asking, "I just heard that you are getting a divorce. Is that true? Can I help you make sure you are following Christ's commands in this difficult time?" Now what?

My Thoughts on how I could/should respond

<u>Gary's Thoughts</u>

Begin with, "I think I can understand some of your frustrations. You feel like you've been left alone to deal with all this pain. I am truly sorry that I hadn't noticed that your marriage was falling apart earlier. I know that my stepping in then would have been more caring and helpful. Would you please forgive me for not being more attentive to whatever signals you sent asking for my help?" This apology, if accepted, can then be followed up with, "Are you sure I can't stand with you in this hard situation?"

If they are unwilling or non-responsive, there really is not much more we can do. Since this man claims to be a Christ-follower, it is important that we make clear the biblical truth, spoken in love. This includes truth about his divorce and whether he has the freedom to remarry.

The frustration of this elder is that he, and the rest of the elders, are being held accountable for not helping, even though they just found out about the situation.

People in hard marriages often assume many other people know their struggles. Or, they are sure someone they have VENTED to will pass on the info, even though that would be GOSSIP.

Without ESCALATING the conflict per MATTHEW 18 principles, rarely will anyone feel empowered to "stick their noses in another person's business." Divorce always becomes public, since it is registered at the court house. But, if this is when the elders or other leaders find out, it is often too late. The decision to divorce and the assumption of the right to remarry is solidified in most folks' minds, even when there has been no sexual immorality or desertion by an unbeliever.

This individual, if there are any signs of a tender heart, could be asked, "Do you think that the biblical grounds for a divorce include not feeling loved?"

More firm CARE-FRONTING may include, "Since you claim to be a Christian, as does your wife, did you ESCALATE your confrontation of her sin per MATTHEW 18 steps? If you tried, I as an elder in our church should have known."

"I know I am being firm, but I want you to live under the smile of God's blessing. I am willing to help you process of this as a brother in Christ. If you refuse my help, I believe God still requires that you deal with these questions."

<u>Prayerful Reflection</u>

Ask God to bring to your mind conflicts you have been in or know about. What insights from this case study could be applied? Additionally, are there concepts and strategies that you did not originally consider, but now realize you need to incorporate into your thinking?

CASE STUDY 15

"They left without saying goodbye. That's just plain rudeness. So why do I have to try one more time to bridge the gap between us? Why do I have to be the one to extend my hand one more time? If they wanted reconciliation and peace, they would have stuck around to work on things."

After talking with your pastor about someone whose absence had become obvious to you, you get this response. How can you be a peacemaker in this situation?

My Thoughts on how I could/should respond

173

Gary's Thoughts

Pastors are not immune to dealing with conflict poorly. People are often rude, as expressed in leaving the church without saying a word. This is often taken very personally by the pastor. It seems that this pastor may need help in FIGHTING FOR THE JUDGMENT OF CHARITY.

We can ask him whether we can brainstorm with him the MOTIVES that might explain why someone might leave a church without saying anything first. Perhaps they were too intimidated to talk things through. Maybe they thought they wouldn't be missed anyway, so why make a fuss. It could be that they thought this was the best way to not be a "trouble-maker."

As we ask the Holy Spirit to help us regain some measure of the JUDGMENT OF CHARITY, we then can go back to the pastors' questions. Though he asked the questions rhetorically, we can ask him to reflect by asking, "What do you think Jesus would say to the Christian who doesn't want to go first, or to go again?" He, most likely, already knows the answers but needs to remind himself of the truth of Who he is following.

While we can express EMPATHY about the pain he is experiencing, we must also give encouragement that helps him see the need to OPEN HIS HAND toward the other people. First, in his heart. And then, in his actions. Suffering for and with Christ includes living with AN OPEN HAND to all others.

Note that he may not understand the difference between the EXTENDED, OPEN HAND OF FORGIVENESS and the two hands clasping one another in the COMPLETED FORGIVENESS of reconciliation. It may be helpful to explain the differences to him.

It is appropriate to offer to pray with and for him. Ask, "Is there anything I can do, beyond prayer, to help you try one more time and make sure you are at peace with all men, as much as it depends on you?"

Prayerful Reflection

Ask God to bring to your mind conflicts you have been in or know about. What insights from this case study could be applied? Additionally, are there concepts and strategies that you did not originally consider, but now realize you need to incorporate into your thinking?

CASE STUDY 16

You've tried to mediate between the two sides. It has gotten ugly, with threats to take it to the courts. There is so much "he said, she said" that you can hardly make sense of even the basic timeline of events. The trust-level is almost nil. There are time pressures. What would you suggest as a way forward?

My Thoughts on how I could/should respond

Gary's Thoughts

The Scriptures warn us, as followers of Jesus, to not take our conflicts to the secular courts. The Apostle Paul reprimands the church at Corinth for allowing it to happen. He chides them by asking whether there are not capable people to make a judgment within the believers (see 1 Corinthians 6).

The challenge is not whether there are people wise enough to make a judgment call, but whether there is the humility on the part of those involved to submit to such a judgment. Many of us struggle to give up control by agreeing to abide by the decision of arbiter. BINDING ARBITRATION sounds fine until the judgment is not in your favor.

When we deal with conflict between two groups, things often get very complicated. There may be personal conflicts that lie behind or within the group conflicts. Finding the best answer for both groups may not address the hurts found in the individuals within those groups.

If there is a clear PRESENTING ISSUE that both groups agree the biggest stumbling block to peace, and all efforts to find common group have yielded no fruit, then proposing binding mediation is an option we can bring forth.

We must make clear that both sides would need to agree to who the arbiter or judge would be. This would also include how many would be involved (usually not more than three). Both sides would be allowed to present their arguments and give a rebuttal to what is said by the others.

We should ask both sides to sign a document declaring that they will abide by the decision of the judge/arbiter. If they are not formal groups, with a recognized leader, this would include the signatures of all involved.

It is at this point that some will bolt. If they do, then we must CARE-FRONT them with the 1 Corinthian 6 teaching. We must so PURSUE PEACE that we are even willing to be defrauded rather than bring dishonor to the name of Jesus.

If they will not either participate in the arbitration OR recommend another way forward toward peace, then we must ESCALATE the conflict per MATTHEW 18 steps. To not follow the teaching from 1 Corinthians 6 is to actively choose to sin.

Prayerful Reflection

Ask God to bring to your mind conflicts you have been in or know about. What insights from this case study could be applied? Additionally, are there concepts and strategies that you did not originally consider, but now realize you need to incorporate into your thinking?

GLOSSARY FOR CASE STUDIES

ACCOUNTABILITY – the process of asking for specific action steps that someone promises to take and by when they will be done. The mediator then holds the party responsible for those action steps by the agreed upon time. If the action steps are not done, then the mediator, as well as the other party, has been sinned against. The mediator is now a direct witness of the sin of lying and should care-front accordingly.

BINDING ARBITRATION – the agreement between two or more parties to submit to the judgment of a neutral arbiter or judge (or panel of judges). This is used when there are time pressures and threats of taking the conflict to the secular courts. It is an expression of putting into practice what is taught in 1 Corinthians 6:1-8.

CARE-FRONTING – this is David Augsburger's coined word for "caring enough to confront." It is a helpful reminder that confronting a perceived problem in a relationship is an expression of caring.

CHECKING IT OUT – because of Filters, both theirs and ours, it is almost impossible to have communication without assumptions. Checking It Out is the process of clarifying if the assumptions we see present are accurate or need to be reassessed.

CLEAN WOUND – conflict wounds us but the real danger is when the cut becomes inflected. Dealing with the injury, using biblical principles of care-fronting and forgiveness, allows us to have a disinfected wound. God is the only One Who can heal any wound, but we have the responsibility to get rid of the infections of bitterness and resentment.

COMPLETED FORGIVENESS (RECONCILIATION) – this is the ultimate goal for conflict resolution for a follower of Jesus. To have the hand of Extended Forgiveness clasp the hand of Extended Repentance in a renewed relationship of joy and peace, that is what we must work toward.

CYCLE OF CONFLICT – the typical pattern that extended conflict follows. Stage one is SOMETHING'S WRONG. It is marked by the development of tension, yet with an uncertainty of the specific issue at hand. Stage two is WHAT'S WRONG. The conflict now has a clearly defined issue at stake. Stage three is the first dangerous stage. YOU'RE WRONG changes the focus from the issue to the other person. The transition point from stage two to three is usually marked by the beginning of Injustice Gathering. This seeks to provide further "proof" that the other person is the real problem. The transition is also marked by the loss of the Judgment of Charity toward the other person's motives. Stage four is LET'S FIGHT. Often triggered by a Presenting Issue, the on-going conflict is not confronted. This explosion will vary in size depending on how long the third stage has been going on. The "fight" here may end up in some sort of resolution, stage five, or may be fed into the Death Spiral and continue with further injustice gathering. The fifth stage is also called, WHO WON?

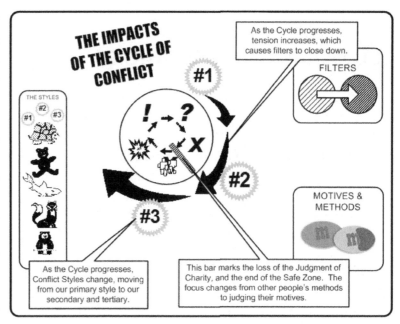

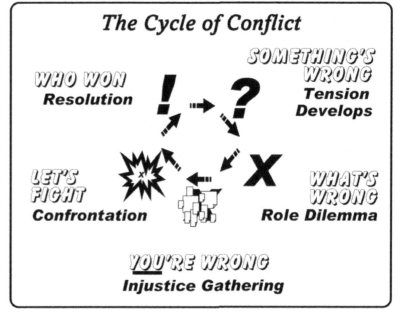

DEATH SPIRAL – the vortex of on-going conflict that is not well resolved. Though the conflict exploded, stage four of the Cycle, there was no helpful resolution. Therefore, the conflict spirals back into stage three, which focuses on finding more evidence for why the other person is really the problem. Sharks and Foxes sometimes think they have "won" the conflict but the other party merely gives in for the moment and then retreats to further gather injustices.

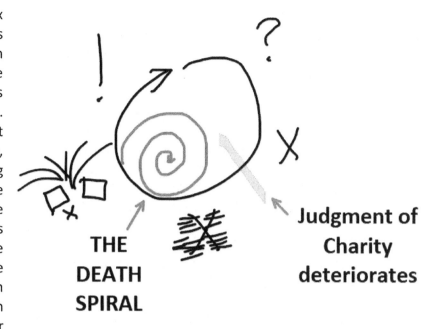

THE DEATH SPIRAL

Judgment of Charity deteriorates

EMPATHY – identifying with the feelings or attitudes that a person may have. We can seek to understand and even by sympathetic to someone's Motives, without assuming that they therefore have the warrant to act out in unbiblical Methods.

ESCALATE (ESCALATION) – in the context of conflict, this is the stepping up of the urgency level of dealing with the issue. The steps are based mainly on Matthew 18:15-20. We first go the least threat level possible, that is, one on one. Then we take one or two others along. Finally, if resolution still has not taken place, we take it to the church. Steps of escalation often exist in the workplace as well, even if not distinctively Christian. When escalating conflict with a professing Christian, the end result for a non-repentant individual is to have the church declare them to be an unbeliever. This declaration has binding authority, even in heaven (see verses 18-20).

EXTENDED (OFFERED) FORGIVENESS – letting go of all clamor, slander, and wrath, we offer or extend forgiveness to everyone. We turn over judgment to God, leaving room for His vengeance. This means that we are not prisoners of other people's choices, to repent or not. This important aspect of forgiveness must not be confused with the hopeful goal of conflict resolution, Completed Forgiveness.

EXTENDED (OFFERED) REPENTANCE – when we have wronged someone else, we should repent in our hearts (which God sees) and then in our actions. Whether the other person chooses to forgive us is not up to us. If the other party professes to be a follower of Jesus and they will not forgive us, they have sinned against the teaching of Luke 17:3-4, "Pay attention to yourselves! If your brother sins, rebuke him, and if he repents, forgive him, and if he sins against you seven times in the day, and turns to you seven times, saying, 'I repent,' you must forgive him."

FILTERS – all of our communication, both sent and received, goes through the gridwork of our pasts, our sinful selves that quickly gives ourselves the judgment of charity, and our self-talk. It is impossible to not have filters but being aware of them helps us to listen better and to speak for greater understanding.

FOX – a style of dealing with conflict that focuses on negotiation. The difference between a Fox and an Owl, is that the Owl will be open about what their goals are. The Fox usually holds their cards close to the vest. The Fox says, "Let's do it HALF MY WAY and HAVE YOUR WAY." In the long-term, it is hard to trust the Fox. One feels like we are always bartering for the best deal. Under time pressures, this may be the only style that gets to a reasonable resolution. As with all the styles, they tend to change depending on the tension level within the conflict.

FRUITS OF REPENTANCE – the outward, visible, tangible changed behaviors that result from Repentance in one's heart. The continued presence of "fresh fruit" helps others' gain trust that we have really repented.

GOSSIP – occurs when three conditions exist. (1) Talking bad about someone, (2) who is not present (behind their backs), and (3) not for the purpose of seeking reconciliation and peace. The third condition allows for "talking bad behind someone's back" if we are seeking counsel for how to approach that person, in order to Care-front them about the "bad" they have done. Matthew Mitchell's Resisting Gossip: Winning the War of the Wagging Tongue, was foundational for the first two of these three warning sirens. I changed the third one because Mitchell had "out of a bad heart," and I think we all have such an ability to rationalize and justify ourselves, that we will give ourselves the judgment of charity and think almost nothing we do is "out of a bad heart."

INJUSTICE GATHERING – the title given by Norm Shawchuck for the third stage of conflict. Also called YOU'RE WRONG. The focus changes from assuming the best Motives on the other person's part, to questioning whether they are not the heart of the problem. This usually involves assuming that they have bad Motives behind their Methods.

JUDGMENT OF CHARITY – this is active choice to entrust ultimate judgment about someone's motives to God, to lower our own self defenses, and to make a way by assuming the very best motives possible behind their methods. This follows the acronym ELM (Entrust, Lower, Make a Way).

MATTHEW 18 – refers to Jesus' teaching on what to do if your brother sins against you. This involves both the Escalation of conflict and the willingness to forgive seventy-seven times (sometimes renders seventy times seven).

METHODS – the external, visible actions that can be witnessed by others. We are accountable for our methods even if our motives seem good. Unintentional sin is when our methods are sinful, though we did not intentional choose to sin.

MIND-READING – the faulty assumption that I can read someone else's mind, or they can read mine. In practice, this is often the assumption that I can know another person's Motives apart from the Methods of communication used to share them with me. Or, that others should be able to know my intentions or Motives even if I do not actively communicate them with my words.

MOTIVES – the heart intentions that only God knows perfectly. Even an individual cannot know for certain their own motives, as the Apostle Paul says in 1 Corinthians 4:4, "For I am not aware of anything against myself, but I am not thereby acquitted. It is the Lord who judges me."

OPEN HAND – the illustration that challenges Christ-followers to always work toward living with open hands, whether open in Extending Forgiveness or in Extending Repentance. This in contrast to a hand "closed" with anger and bitterness.

OWL – a style of dealing with conflict that seeks to speak the truth in love. The wise Owl believes that, in the long-term, the best way to deal with conflicts is to collaborate. Thus, they say, "Let's do it OUR WAY." An Owl manifests the strength of a Shark but also the gentleness of a Teddy Bear. The only style that we can engage with that will encourage others to be an Owl, is to be an Owl ourselves.

PIGEON-HOLING – the short-cut in our thinking that puts people into boxes or categories based on their Methods. Often this includes the use of our Filters to decide, without careful consideration, that people whose Methods are a certain way must fit in one of our boxes or stereotypes. These usually come with corresponding assumptions about others' Motives.

PRESENTING ISSUE – the "final straw that breaks the camel's back" and moves the conflict from stage three to stage four. After an extended time of Injustice Gathering in the You're Wrong stage, the Let's Fight stage often is started over some small issue. To an outsider, this "sin" can seem inconsequential and one that should be easily overlooked. But, to the person who has been stewing in bitterness, gathering evidence that the other person is really the problem, this trespass is the final bit of evidence they need to finally "let them have it."

REPENTANCE – the change of heart, turning from sin and turning to God and His will. God sees whether repentance in the heart is real. We cannot know for certain if it is genuine until it expresses itself in the Fruits of Repentance. True repentance will ALWAYS manifest itself with fruit.

SHARK – a style of dealing with conflict that sees conflict as a competition, with winners and losers. The shark will assert itself to be the victor. Some sharks may see themselves as "benevolent dictators," but nevertheless, their Methods usually come across to others as controlling. The Shark says, "Let's do it MY WAY." The long-term impact of this style is to swim alone, perhaps feeling justified in our decisions because people often give in to us. As with all the styles, they tend to change depending on the tension level within the conflict.

SINS AND RESENTMENTS LIST – the exercise of the parties who have been involved in ongoing conflict that seeks to "clean the slate." Each party is asked to prayerfully spend time alone with God, asking Him to help them write down the sins they have committed against the other party, as well as the resentments they have toward the other party. The parties then get together, usually in the presence of a mediator, and share their lists. They begin with the confession of their sins, asking for forgiveness for each one. Then the lists of resentments are shared, minus the items that have been already confessed. The end result, if done humbly under the Spirit's guidance, will be no unconfessed or unforgiven sins between them. The mediator will also be able to recommend specific actions that will help them rebuild trust by manifesting the fruits of repentance in the near future.

STYLES OF CONFLICT – the five basic modes of dealing with conflict that reflect varying emphasis on Truth and Love. These two tensions could also be labeled "Goals" and "Relationships." The first tension reflects how assertive we are in presenting and defending our goals or what we consider "true." The second tension is how responsive we are to others and our desire for an ongoing relationship with them. The styles are Turtle, Teddy Bear, Shark, Fox, and Owl (definitions for each are found separately in this glossary).

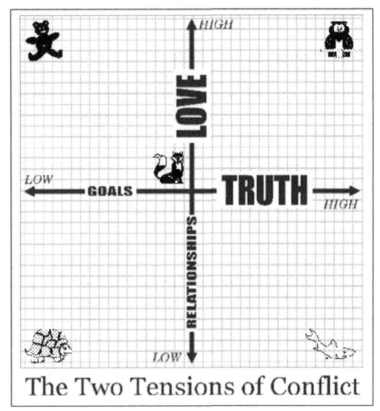

The Two Tensions of Conflict

TEDDY BEAR – a style of dealing with conflict that is known for its accommodation of the other party's goals. The Teddy Bear cares more for the relationship than for their goals. The Teddy Bear says, "Let's do it YOUR WAY." The long-term impact of this style is for others to assume we will go along with anything, as long as you invite us along. As with all the styles, they tend to change depending on the tension level within the conflict.

TIME-OUT – a simple tool for helping conflict be dealt with productively. When all the parties agree to use it, any of them can call a "time out." This stops "the game" and gives opportunity to re-group. Christians can agree that when a time out is called that they will join hands, and all will pray that God would help them, with each individual's prayer focused on their own actions. This process invites the Holy Spirit into the conflict. It also helps the more timid or less assertive person have a way to communicate that they feel they are getting "run over."

TRUTH IN LOVE – from Ephesians 4:15, describing what must happen for a diverse church to operate in unity. Literally, "truthing in love." These are the two tensions in conflict. As followers of Jesus, we are mandated to hold to both.

TURTLE – a style of dealing with conflict that avoids. Pulling into whatever protective shell they have, the turtle allows others to make decisions. Their lack of active involvement will tend to make them withdraw from relationship in general. The Turtle says, "NO WAY am I doing this." Long-term, people tend to ignore the turtle because they are seen as those who will not actively get involved. As with all the styles, they tend to change depending on the tension level within the conflict.

TWO HANDS OF FORGIVENESS – a model using two hands to show how the forgiveness between two people should be modeled on the forgiveness of God for those who repent and believe. This model allows for the differentiation between Extended Forgiveness, Extended Repentance, and Completed Forgiveness (Reconciliation).

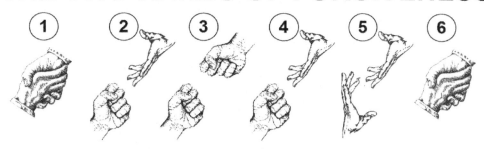

THE TWO HANDS OF FORGIVENESS

1. We were created to have fellowship with our Creator.

2. But we chose to sin and rebel against God (shaking our fist at Him).

3. And the Holy Perfect God was righteously angry with us for our rebellion. He closed His fist in judgment of our sin.

4. But God so loved us that He extended forgiveness (opening His hand) to the whole world through the work of His Son, Jesus. Yet that does not mean that the whole world is forgiven. God honors us by giving us a choice. We must respond in order to be forgiven.

5. We open our hand to receive God's gift by turning away from our sin in repentance and asking for forgiveness, trusting by faith in the work of Jesus.

6. Now the forgiveness is "complete" because we are reconciled to God in restored fellowship with Him as our Creator and Redeemer.

VENTING – the common excuse for gossip when talking about others behind their backs. Gossip is present because there is no request or offer of help to go deal with the problem. "I just need to 'vent' a bit so that I can go back and face the pressure some more." Such a statement often comes from Turtles or Teddy Bears who do not think they can care-front the problem. Yet, they feel an obligation to stay in the relationship. Doing so is pressuring them into changing the conflict style, perhaps to that of a Shark, which is something they do not want to do.

WHAT'S WRONG – the second stage in the Cycle of Conflict. The last safe stage, when the focus is still on the issue of the Methods at the heart of the conflict.

YOU'RE WRONG – the third stage of the Cycle of Conflict. This is the dangerous stage that must be avoided by dealing with conflict before the sun goes down. In this stage the focus changes from the other person's Methods to their Motives.

WORKSHOP PREPERATION INSTRUCTIONS

For those using this workbook as part of a workshop, please make the following preparations for the time you will spend together with your instructor and fellow peacemakers.

- ☐ Read through the **Core Commitments** and **Biblical Foundations**. *You should be able to recall the Five Commitments using the acronym PEACE.*

- ☐ Decide if you will commit yourself to the Core Commitments. If not, then this workshop will be of minimal value to you.

- ☐ Study the **One-Page Training Sheets.** For those who have seen some of this material before, a brief review may be all you need. *You should be able to answer all the Pop Quiz questions. Additionally, you should be able to draw and label the Cycle of Conflict, the Two Tensions of Conflict and the Animal Styles, and the Map of Forgiveness.*

- ☐ Be prepared for a <u>pre-workshop test</u> that will review the Core Commitments and One-Page Training Sheet sections. *See the italics in the items above to help guide your study.*

  - ○ When taken for credit, a minimal score of 80% will be required to allow taking the rest of the workshop for credit. Those who score less than 80% can attend the workshop sessions, but no credit will be given.

- ☐ Work through the **Case Studies**, writing down what you think could/should be done, then review Gary's thoughts. Prayerfully consider how insights you have gained may apply to conflicts you have been involved with. These will be discussed during the workshop.

- ☐ <u>Write up two (2) of your own case studies</u>. These should be based on actual situations but with the names and identifying details removed. These are to be written legibly or preferably typed. They will be collected at the first session of the workshop. These will be discussed during the workshop.

ADDITIONAL DISCUSSION QUESTIONS

This is a list of questions that might spur discussion during the workshop sessions:

- ☐ When is it right to separate from other believers?
- ☐ Why is staff conflict among the most painful experiences of pastors in a larger church?
- ☐ When is it right to submit? When is it wrong?
- ☐ Why do issues that we thought were solved keep coming up again and again?
- ☐ How can we have a difficult discussion profitably?
- ☐ Why is conflict management by email or text is usually a terrible choice?
- ☐ How can we provide a meaningful review without being mean? (Integrating leadership values and capacity)
- ☐ What does it mean to operate from consensus?
- ☐ How can we guard the gate with red, yellow, and green lights?
- ☐ When is it time to ask for a mediator's help?
- ☐ Do we want a mediator, a judge, a detective, or a hit-man?
- ☐ How is pride behind so many failed attempts at reconciliation?
- ☐ When should someone be labeled "a decisive person?" (Titus 3:10)
- ☐ When should we defend ourselves and when should we "just stand there and take it?"
- ☐ Should we church discipline those who are only regular attenders and not actual members?
- ☐ Do we have to do a psychological exploration of our motives, and theirs, every time?
- ☐ Is it OK to end a relationship with a fellow-believer?

SELECT BIBLIOGRAPHY

Though many books have influenced my thinking on this subject over the past 30 years, the following were specifically referred to in the workbook:

Augsburger, David. <u>Caring Enough to Confront</u>. Ventura CA: Regal Books, 1984.

Augsburger, David. <u>Caring Enough to Forgive/Not Forgive</u>. Ventura CA: Regal Books, 1985.

Inrig, Gary. <u>Forgiveness</u>. Grand Rapids MI: Discovery House Publishers, 2005.

Shawchuck, Norman. <u>How to Manage Conflict in the Church.</u> Volumes 1 and 2. Indianapolis IN: Spiritual Growth Resources, 1983.

Made in the USA
Coppell, TX
08 September 2021